# Through Death to Life

# Through Death
## to
## Life

**Ron Gries**

Proctor Publication, LLC
Ann Arbor, Michigan, USA

Proctor Publications, LLC
P.O. Box 2498
Ann Arbor, Michigan 48106
800-343-3034
Printed in the United States of America

Publisher's Cataloging-in-Publication
*(Provided by Quality Books, Inc.)*

Gries, Ronald.
   Through death to life / by Ron Gries. --1$^{st}$ ed.
   p. cm.
   LCCN: 99-75096
   ISBN: 1-882792-87-4

   1. Grief--Religious aspects--Christianity.
   2. Bereavement--Religious aspects--Christianity.
   3. Grief--Religious aspects--Christianity--Poetry.
   4. Bereavement--Religious aspects--Christianity--
Poetry.   I. Title.

BV4905.2.G75 1999                     242'.4
                               QB199-1415

## *DEDICATION*

This book is dedicated
to those nearing the end of their life,
and the loved ones who care for them,
as they strive to make sense
of their earthly existence
and the promise of the eternal.
It is written in memory
of the one who taught me so much
about life, love, spirituality, and courage.

Patty Gries
1941 - 1997

## *ACKNOWLEDGMENTS*

First I would like to thank Joyce DeShano, ssj who conceived the idea for this book after reading a number of my poems, and convinced me that my story could help others. She was also a strong voice in improving the work and provided much needed support for a sometimes unsure writer. Mary Lindquist has my thanks for a wonderful job of timely editing to bring out the best in the writing, and I acknowledge Sandra Marshall and Elaine Grohman for their helpful suggestions. I am indebted to Hazel Proctor, my publisher, who showed remarkable patience in helping a first-time author through the maze of publishing. I am also indebted to Hospice of Michigan who provided physical, emotional, and spiritual support for our family during the last months of Patty's life and continue to offer me comfort and encouragement.

I will never forget the love and support that Patty and I received from relatives, friends, and neighbors through the long struggle. You will meet a few of them in these pages but there are far too many to mention, a tribute to the abundance of love that exists in our world.

Lastly, I would like to thank Cathy, Doug, and Laura, the legacy of my journey with Patty, who fill me with pride and constantly remind me that I am still very much blessed.

I do not believe that sheer suffering teaches. If suffering alone taught, all the world would be wise, since everyone suffers. To suffering must be added mourning, understanding, patience, love, openness, and the willingness to remain vulnerable.

-Anne Morrow Lindbergh

Give sorrow words the grief that does not speak whispers the oe'r fraught heart and bids it break.

-William Shakespeare

Whoever survives a test, whatever it might be, must tell the story. That is his duty.

-Elie Wiesel

# CONTENTS

## PROLOGUE

This book chronicles a personal journey that began with the doctor's sad words advising us that my wife Patty's medullary thyroid cancer, that had been in relative remission for many years, had now spread to her bones. We already knew that there was no cure possible if this occurred. The answer to the obvious question, "How long do I have?" was "Less than five years." It turned out to be three and a half.

The book will cover caregiving, the last days, and grieving. I wrote in poetic form throughout her ordeal and for more than a year after she died, simply to help myself better understand what was happening, and to get in touch with my feelings during an extraordinary part of my life. Most of the writing was done soon after particular emotions were triggered. It came from a very deep part of me that housed feelings stronger than I had ever known. I would hope that in these words you might be able to explore similar feelings, possibly learning more about yourself and your relationship with loved ones. While no two of us are exactly alike, I believe that we share more feelings and emotions than most of us can talk about. It is only in my witnessing Patty's terrible ordeal and reflecting on its meaning that I found the freedom to share my most personal thoughts.

Some of the poems will make reference to God or the Light or the One. It makes no difference to me how any individual relates to a higher power, for I believe that to be a most personal matter. But regardless of any religious affiliation, one central fact became very clear to me through our great trial. Without a strong belief in a loving God, and the promise of eternal life with Him, I don't know how Patty and I would have been able to endure and work through the anguish and despair to a relatively calm and peaceful conclusion.

# HISTORY

In 1983 my wife Patty, at age 42, was diagnosed with malignant medullary thyroid cancer, a relatively rare and serious cancer. Medical treatment involved removing the cancerous thyroid. This particular cancer has a tendency to spread to lungs and bone through the lymph system but there was no evidence of spreading at this time and we were very optimistic. Because this cancer is very slow growing, chemotherapy would not be effective and was not an option. The plan was simply to monitor the lymph nodes in the neck area for any cancerous growth. No problems were encountered until 1990 when malignant lymph nodes were discovered. They were removed surgically and the process repeated again in 1992. At this point the prognosis became much less encouraging but there was still hope for remission. During this time period Patty was also diagnosed with fibromyalgia, a little understood rheumatism-like disease of the soft tissue that causes severe pain, fatigue, sleeplessness and a host of other symptoms. The pain is unique in that conventional pain relief medication is not effective. Patty was now facing a double dose of pain and anxiety.

As for my part in chronicling this saga, the evolution of this book can be traced to a decision I made in the fall of 1993 to sign up for a once-a-week community education class in creative writing. The class provided the discipline I needed to write, along with the opportunity to record my reaction to her great struggle. It still amazes me that the inspiration to write occurred exactly when I needed so badly to understand what I was feeling. Along the way I learned a lot about myself, our relationship with each other and our God, and the abundance and power of human love.

# Through Death
## to
# Life

**Book One**

*A TIME FOR CAREGIVING*

## The Beginning of the End

In September of 1993, we were scheduled for a routine quarterly monitoring visit with Dr. Norman Thompson, a recognized authority on medullary thyroid cancer at the University of Michigan Hospital. He had become Patty's doctor some years earlier and had performed the surgeries in 1990 and 1992. On each occasion he told us quite honestly that there were probably more infected lymph nodes that he simply could not find which could spread the cancer. But we had been encouraged by the results of the quarterly examinations and lab tests. However, lately she had been experiencing some increased pain so a complete bone scan had been done. During this visit we would get the results.

It was very quiet in the car during the one hour trip to Ann Arbor. On previous visits over the years our optimism would produce the easy banter and laughs that we enjoyed. But today was different. We started out with nervous words of confidence but they soon gave way to increased silence. I wanted to give her assurances that the scans would prove negative. I had hoped and prayed for so long that the cancer wouldn't spread. But deep down I was not feeling confident. I was just scared. And after thirty four years of marriage I wasn't going to fool her. So I said little as my mind raced with thoughts of unpleasant consequences.

In the small examining room at the doctor's office, Patty sat nervously twisting a tissue while I paced. She finally asked me to sit down, shortly before the door opened.

## THE DOCTOR'S WORDS

He is an expert in his field,
       but just as importantly,
       a kindly man.
He is not a young man,
       but his hands are sure,
       his knowledge superior,
       and he cares.
We knew always that we would wait
       after our appointed time,
       but with him it didn't matter.
We knew that we would not be rushed,
       that he would give us all he could
       until we were satisfied.
Sometimes, when our appointment
       was late in the day,
       I could see the fatigue in his eyes.
But he would still smile,
       and he would stay with us
       as long as we needed him.

When he walked into the room
       on that September day,
       I knew what he would say
       when I looked into his eyes,
       even before he spoke.

4

I saw more than fatigue there.
I saw pain.
When he gave us the news,
      that Patty's time was limited
      by the cancer spread to the bones,
      His voice was soft and sad.
Patty was disconsolate.
She told him of her plans
      for when I retired in five years,
      of her work begun on designing
      the new home for us.
She asked, "What should I do?"
      "How long do I have?"
He gave her the news
      in words that I won't forget,
"By all means continue your planning.
Just don't pay any architects."
It was the kindest way he could tell us
      that our life together
      now had a foreseeable end.

## SHOCK

What is there to say?
The words are so final.
Medical science has spoken.
Barring a miracle,
    she will not survive
    to enjoy the retirement
    we were planning.
We knew it could happen,
    and probably would some day,
    but still we are not prepared.
It is an awkward time.
The optimism that has carried us
    for such a long time
    has now been replaced
    by some impersonal X-Rays
    and an expert's opinion.
This is not like a jury verdict.
There is no appeal process.
There is no mistake
    in the proceedings
    that can produce
    a different decision.
X-Rays don't lie.
Barring a miracle,
    which we both believe can happen,
    our time together
    has now been fixed,
    and our lives
    will never be the same.

## The First Year of the Rest of Her Life

The first year of the struggle saw the cancer spread very little while the pain of the fibromyalgia got worse. We wondered how many vacations were left for us so we splurged and rented a condo in Florida for the month of March. An avid golfer, Patty was still able to play but her strength was noticeably diminished. Our three adult children joined us at times during the month and we had a good time. It did turn out to be our last vacation.

By summertime golf was no longer possible. The fibromyalgia, together with the cancer, had weakened her enough that the exertion was just too much. It was at this point that her spirits nosedived with the loss of golfing and the increased pain. We began to explore our life together and our future. We talked hope. We talked remission. We talked miracle. And we prayed. But the pain just got worse. And the special laugh that was so much a part of her mostly disappeared. That laugh was one of the great things about her that first attracted me. She had a wonderful sense of humor and, since I had always been an imagined stand up comedian, it was a vital part of our marriage. To see her pain increase and her laughter disappear was so sad for me. I could not even imagine how difficult it was for her. And the worst part of all for me was my utter and complete helplessness. I could comfort, I could assist, I could listen. I could work harder and longer than I ever had before. But I could not "fix" the disease. And I couldn't stop the horrible pain.

## LAUGHTER LOST

I think I miss her laugh the most.
The illness has robbed us of that treat.
Uncertainty and pain have conspired
    to make real laughing impossible.

That special laughter
    would start slowly,
    the eyes giving the first hint,
    brightening noticeably,
    and growing larger
    in anticipation.
Then the mouth would begin,
    first just at the edges,
    a crinkling causing little lines
    to speed slowly to the cheeks.
The lines would deepen
    as the lips parted into a faint smile,
    then a grin, and finally a full laugh,
    with the accompanying sounds
    that couldn't be contained.
Then, as if on cue, the tears would come,
    cascading down reddened cheeks
    until small rivers were formed.
Soon the rush for the tissue
    to stem the tide,
    even as she doubled over
    when the breathing couldn't contain
    the joy.

I think I miss her laugh the most.
But deep down where my truth lies
        the memory is still fresh.
I know it will arise again one day,
        when the battle is won,
        the spirit renewed,
        and the world offers her
        the opportunity to laugh.

## PAIN

I watch her struggle,
> her face betraying the first signs.
The pain is coming again.
Now her eyes plead for help.
They silently ask for the signs to be wrong,
> hoping it is a mistake.
But there is no mistake.
Pain advances quickly
> from the neck to the back,
> now racing down into the hips.
Quickly I race for the medicine
> that really only dulls slightly
> the awful pain.
I watch from so close,
> and yet from afar,
> wanting to help,
> but so powerless
> against the onslaught
> that now consumes her.
I hold her hand,
> mumble words to help
> that I know do little
> to halt the pain
> that she will endure
> so quietly,
> so patiently,
> until it lessens,
> and comfort returns,
> until the next time.

## Self Exploration

In late '94 my Creative Writing instructor gave us an assignment to write something strictly about ourselves. The turmoil in our lives was evident in the two poems that I wrote a week apart. Without even mentioning Patty directly I was setting my course for the coming trials. I would rely on God's love to give me what I needed for my journey and try to be accepting of myself and our situation.

It was during this time period that at some level I decided not to become a self proclaimed martyr to Patty's illness. My focus would be on doing the best that I could each day to take care of her, helping her to find whatever measure of comfort, peace and pleasure that was possible, while doing enough for myself to stay mentally and physically healthy. I was preparing myself for a long struggle that would no doubt test us in ways that I could not even imagine. I knew that I had to try to keep my equilibrium if I were to be the right kind of caregiver. I did not want anyone to feel sorry for me because of what Patty's illness had done to our lives. I would just try to make each day the best that it could be for her and for me. To my best recollection there were only two times during her long ordeal that I actually broke down. Both times happened at work in private conversations with co-workers when the enormity of our situation engulfed me and I could not keep myself together.

## ME

I have often wondered what it is
        that sends my mood soaring like an eagle
        one day, and the very next plummets it on
        the rocks.
One day I am joy, hope, love.
The next I am doubt, sadness, insecurity.
And on a third, somewhere lost in between.
Am I just one person?
Or am I two, or even three,
        trying to coexist in one earthly body.
If I take the time to still my mind
        and really explore my own being,
        to dig until my life is exposed
        like some album of dated photographs,
        the answer comes.
I AM ME!
There is no other like me.
And there is a God that loves me totally,
        through joy and sadness,
        triumph and failure,
        hope and fear,
        love and hate.
My journey is totally unique.
It has never been done by another soul,
        and will never be repeated.
All I need do is live it
        with the gifts and burdens I have been
        given,
        try to make myself a better person today
        than I was yesterday,

try to help others along the way,
and be true to the teachings
that were first given life
two thousand years ago
and remain just as valid today.

## WHO AM I?

I find life terribly confusing sometimes.
Is it really so complicated,
      or do I make it that way
      because of this spastic mind
      that often has trouble
      remembering and focusing?
I didn't choose to have this mind
      that seems to race itself
      with scattered thoughts
      and disconnected ideas.
At times my confusion gives way to anger,
      but at what - or whom?
Even that is difficult to know sometimes.
Other times my confusion
      gives way to apathy and withdrawal.
Then I let some precious earth time
      slip by without caring enough.
That is when I can become so alone.
But most of the time
      I see the value of my struggle
      to make sense of my existence,
      to learn and grow at my own pace.
It is not an easy lesson to learn,
      but oh the reward
      to know that I can overcome
      this private handicap,

that the many gifts I have been given
far exceed the small hindrances,
and that I can take pride in who I am
and what I have accomplished.
It is a blessing indeed,
knowing that my spirit is whole,
my path is clear,
and the future,
while most uncertain,
is my very own adventure to live.

## Dance

Patty had always been a marvelous dancer. It was as much a part of her as life itself. Her body had a particular grace that needed to be expressed. I was just fair, but in my arms she made us both look good. She could read my somewhat unorthodox moves and react so quickly that she appeared to be moving even before I decided where. And if no one was available to dance with her when the dance gods beckoned she would simply create a dance for one.

When her strength noticeably suffered in late '94 there was no more impromptu dancing in our house, until one Sunday morning when she was suffering on the couch while we talked. What happened next was so extraordinary that, when she finished and returned to the couch, I rushed for my pad and the words just leaped onto the page.

She would not dance like that again.

## LAST DANCE

She lies on the couch,
  pain showing in her eyes,
  her weakened body terse.
The remote is aimed
  and the music starts.
First just a quiet beat,
  that slowly builds,
  until the sound invades the body,
  chasing away the pain.
Then the voices begin,
  singing of a lost love.
The harmony speaks to the soul
  and her body responds.
She slowly rises
  and begins to sway,
  awkward and tentative at first,
  as if discovering a lost friend.
Soon she is moving
  with that familiar grace,
  feeling, more than hearing
  the rhythms of life.
She dances to the promise of the music.
There is no pain.
There is no illness.
The music has brought
  its own redemption.
"There is life," it announces.
"There is hope," it boldly proclaims.
And she listens,
  and dreams,
  and smiles.

## Mortality

The sad turn of our lives weighed heavily on me at times as I wondered just how long Patty had to live. Along with those thoughts came a serious consideration of the life cycles that rule us and our ultimate mortality. I thought about the senior status Patty and I had reached, with children raised and on their own, and retirement planning begun. I thought about the satisfaction we had known as we anticipated the pleasant winding down of our busy lives. But it was different now as we faced such a troubling future. I was very much affected by Patty's struggle as I tried to help her deal with serious questions of life, death and eternity. I was also influenced by my older brother Ray and older sister Rosemary who were each courageously battling cancer. Now, as I thought about them and their questionable span of life, a new disturbing thought emerged. How many years might be left for me? Although I was in perfect health I had a sudden sense of foreboding and busied myself getting all of my affairs in order, just in case I didn't survive Patty. I seriously wondered why I should have any right to more years when the good people I was close to had such tenuous futures. So, while I could write about the regular cycles of life at times, the sad nature of our situation was never far from me.

## LIFE

Just as in the first book of Latin,
      where all Gaul is divided into three parts,
      so too is life divided into threes.

The first third is for learning,
      from parents, from teachers, from books,
      from new experiences.
Each event is a first of a kind,
      with the accompanying wonder and awe
      of the awakening senses.
The honing of skills,
      the tasting of the new.

The second third is for doing,
      working at refining the skills
      needed to survive and prosper,
      clarifying the rightful place
      to be taken in society,
      sifting ideas to discover what works,
      accommodating others
      into the private world,
      teaching those that follow.

The last third is for reflecting
      and solidifying,
      with a lessening of responsibilities.

Time for leisure
  and looking at the world
  with an indirect eye.
More thoughts of "why"
  rather than "what" or "how."
More effort at calm and peace
  as life winds down.
The gradual lessening of desire
  as strength ebbs
  and there is more time
  to read,
  to think,
  and to wonder
  about what's to come.

## LIVING

When we are young
    we feel eternal.
Our thoughts are fixed
    or our limitless future.

Love and marriage
    bring a new hope,
    a sharing of destiny,
    as we establish a home
    together.

Children are the richest blessing,
    new lives to nurture,
    to protect,
    to teach,
    to love.

Mid-life is busy,
    career demands,
    children growing,
    learning,
    and then leaving
    to find their place.

Senior status comes soon enough,
    children gone,
    retirement looming,
    more time to ponder life's fortunes,
    and our mortality.

## MORTALITY

I feel her sadness
    filling the room,
    even before she speaks.
The words come softly,
    slowly at first,
    then in a torrent.
The pain has spread.
More bones are involved.
Hope is fighting
    to keep its foothold,
    as the realization grows
    just how tenuous life is
    for her,
    for me,
    and for us.

## Faith

My faith and belief system were bred in me and nurtured by loving parents and Catholic schools. I've been comfortable with my faith and have not seen the need to explore other belief systems. I go to mass at least once a week because I like the church atmosphere and I believe completely in the power of the Eucharist to help me find the peace and joy of my existence and acceptance of life's unpredictable fortune. I pray on my knees every night, first offering thanks for the blessings I have been given. It is a habit learned from my father a long time ago and it has served me well.

At this point I need to explain my thoughts on the difference between spirituality rooted in faith, and religion, a difference Patty illuminated for me. Patty and I were both raised and educated for twelve years in the Catholic Church. Growing up it seems that I was much more interested in following rules of behavior than exploring my spiritual connection with God and the universe, and the infinite power of human and divine love—what I now think of as spirituality. So while I began our marriage more Catholic than spiritual, Patty, unbeknownst even to herself, was quite the opposite. She had more confidence in herself and, some years after our marriage, embarked on a tangent, exploring more deeply her personal relationship with the Universal God she embraced and her own interpretation of the divine plan. I can vividly remember many Sunday mornings when she asked me to stay in communion with her rather than make the obligatory visit to the church. She saw those quiet moments as very spiritual. I didn't disagree with her interpretation, but I could still be bound by duty. Over the years, as we talked and I reflected, I came to understand much of what came so easily to her. I learned that I could be Catholic and expand my spirituality. It was a truly significant awakening for me. Do you wonder why I loved this woman who challenged me more than I often wanted to be challenged?

One morning, as 1994 was moving into 1995 and my spirits were a little low, I experienced the magic of a spiritual moment rooted in my belief system.

## DAYBREAK

The cold slaps me in the face
    as soon as I venture out.
The frost reflecting the early sun
      foretold what the outdoors would offer
      from the warmth of my kitchen.


It is daybreak and the neighborhood sleeps.
My head is stuffed with the imagined onslaught of
    the day.
I feel more tired than refreshed
      as I make the familiar trek for the paper.


I can't help but notice the colorful sky,
    the subtle hues changing even as I watch.
In the west the brilliant three quarter moon
      assures me that the universe is whole.


To the north a small plane makes its ascent,
      its fluffy white tail saying, "Goodbye,"
      while to the south a huge jetliner
      reflects the sun's brilliance
      as it prepares to bring us guests.


The birds in the huge pine
    make note of my intrusion.
The volume of their song
      belies their small stature
      as they unite to speed me away.

As if by magic I no longer feel the cold.
My real and imagined worries are gone,
    temporarily replaced
    by the magic of the moment.
Life still has promise,
    even if limited.
I am alive.
There is a God,
    and He loves me.

## Brothers

In 1993 my older brother Ray, who lived ninety miles away, had been diagnosed with multiple myeloma, a deadly cancer of the bone marrow. Now he was in his second year of chemotherapy, a treatment that ultimately could not save him. His illness was the catalyst for a rebirth of the special closeness that had been missing since we were kids in Cleveland's inner city. Our distance apart, the demands of our families, and markedly different adult interests separated us, while a common love of family, fatherhood, sports and humor did manage to keep us somewhat connected. But things were different now. He was seriously ill and, like Patty, he needed my support. I think that my experience caring for her had sharpened my sensitivity to those like her who were fighting for their lives. When I thought about his situation one day after visiting him during one of his hospital stays, I wrote a poem specifically for him. I'm sure there are many pairs of brothers and other siblings who have traveled a similar road and share some of the same feelings.

Ray died early in 1995. Much later I asked his wife, Helen, about his reaction to my poem. She told me that she read it to him not long before he died, and then he read it himself. She remembered that he was very obviously moved, although he could not find the words to express it. I understood.

## BIG BROTHER

I'm one of the lucky ones.
I have a big brother.
He's been my big brother
    for almost fifty nine years,
    and he'll always be
    my big brother.
I like that.

When we were growing up
    we did everything together,
    city kids playing city games
    and sports on the empty corner lot.
We'd go to the ball park
    to watch the Indians play,
    lugging our sandwiches
    in paper bags.

When my brother went to high school
    we began to separate.
His turf expanded
    out of our cozy neighborhood.
He got a job
    and I didn't see him as much.
The four years age difference
    suddenly seemed much greater.

By the time I went to high school
    he was in college,
    doing college things.
The gap between us widened
    as his time for me shortened.
By now I was finding my own way,
    pursuing the sports that I loved,
    and learning about girls,
    while he talked politics with dad
    and struggled with calculus and working.


I followed him to Case Tech
    and then to Goodyear after graduation.
No doubt the big brother influence
    was very strong.
We lived in the same city
    but didn't share the same friends or interests.
He was into cards, chess, and bowling,
    while learning to be a husband and father.
I was into bachelorhood, graduate school,
    basketball, softball, and volleyball.
My tonic was competition of the body,
    his was more of the mind.
We were both good at what we did.


When I married and then moved away
    the gap between us grew.
He moved shortly after,
    close enough for the occasional visit,
    but far enough away for separation.

There were plenty of family outings
       to bring us together over the years.
I watched him raise his children,
       setting a standard for dedication
       that I hoped to follow.

Just recently we have come full circle,
       close again like it was when we were young,
We're still on opposite sides of many issues,
       but learning how similar we really are
       in the basic nature of our lives,
       and how we wish to live them.

My brother's illness has been the catalyst
       to bring us much closer than we have been.
Maybe it's part of the great plan,
       maybe it's just that we're aging,
       and feeling very mortal.
Why it's happened is not really important.
What is important is that I have a big brother
       that I am proud of
       and that I love.
And for that
       I am very thankful.

## Despair

Through 1995 the cancer slowly spread causing additional pain and the beginnings of despair. Patty had not just been a spectator observing the spread of the cancer. From the first she had actively sought alternative methods for cure since medical science could offer nothing for medullary thyroid cancer. She read voraciously and made contact with a great number of alternative healers, including those who believed fully in the capability of the mind to overcome the body's misadventures. She was well schooled in breathing, meditation, prayer, herbs, diets, hypnosis, and the power of angels, whom she believed sometimes masqueraded as humans. But nothing helped as the cancer advanced and her spirits slowly fell. There were many things that I was skeptical of, but I remained totally supportive of her attempts at healing herself. Through supporting her I learned so much about the powers that we do have over our lives, especially the connection between the physical, mental, and spiritual that we are just now truly validating. I only wish that I could have learned those lessons without the terrible price that she paid for them. And I wish that they could have saved her.

During this time my writing reflected strong feelings as I struggled with her despair and my frustration at not being able to stop her pain and ease her mind.

## SUFFERING

I am mostly a spectator
    and that is the hardest part.
I watch her slipping,
    slowly, steadily, painfully.
I still have the words to say,
    "You will get better,
    you will have a life again,
    you will remember how to laugh."
But she sees through the hollow words.
The signs are too clear.
Her body will not respond
    to her untiring efforts
    and my humble prayer.
She hasn't totally quit her hope.
But she wonders aloud
    in a voice made small by pain,
    "What more can I do?
I've prayed.
I've meditated.
I've read the good messages
    from those who know suffering.
I've done the breathing,
    the herbal healers,
    the positive thinking.
But nothing works as the cancer grows,
    and slowly kills my hope."

For me there is no pain,
> only a deep weariness
> born of frustration with my impotence,
> and raised on her suffering.

"There is a God who loves you," I tell her.
She slowly nods her agreement,
> but then questions His allowing her
> torment.

I tell her that is not for us to know,
> that it's part of a higher plan.

But my weakening conviction is evident
> as I plead with her to persevere,
> for yet another long, painful day.

## NIGHT

It is four o'clock in the morning.
I am awakened by the movement,
    the rustle of the blankets,
    my senses immediately on alert.
The ritual has begun.
She rises slowly, awkwardly,
    her feet searching for the floor.
There is a pause while she summons strength.
Now she rises and shuffles slowly
    toward the dim light of the bathroom.
I note that she did not pause
    to take the drugs
    waiting at her bedside
    for when the pain is too great.
That is a good sign.
It is so still
    as I wait for her return,
    just the odd creak
    from our trusty home.
The loudest noise seems to be
    the beating of my heart,
    although I know
    it is soundless to the world.
Now I hear the familiar noise
    as the trip is completed,
    and the steps return,
    a little quicker this time.

There is no stop for fresh clothing.
Her body has not betrayed her,
    another good sign.
She returns to our bed,
    easing herself back into position,
    protecting the sensitive areas.
The covers are adjusted,
    the breathing slows and deepens.
I reach over and touch lightly.
"Are you OK?" I whisper.
"Yes, I'm fine," she replies.
I let myself relax,
    waiting for sleep to return.
We've had another good night.

## Retirement and Reflection

Halfway through 1995 I wrote a long letter to the kids on a slow day in the office. I had already decided that I would retire at the end of the year. Patty was needing ever increasing attention as the disease progressed and took away more of her mobility, and there were many more mini-crises that meant I had to leave work unexpectedly. I was also unable to travel overnight and this put a burden on the other Goodyear people in my group who had to cover for me. It is to their great credit that they understood my situation and accommodated my particular needs with much sensitivity. There was another serious work issue involved. I just didn't have the interest or the energy anymore to give the job the attention it deserved. I was confronted with a struggle that was close to consuming my life. Facing the death of a loved one will certainly put the importance of the business world in proper perspective. For twenty eight years in Detroit I had prided myself on taking good care of my customers at the auto companies, establishing many solid personal relationships that continue to this day. But now my wife was suffering and facing an almost certain death. My days were too full of struggle and worry to properly take care of our customers, especially the few who could be unreasonable and unprofessional. So I decided to retire at the end of the year. There was some sadness involved in that decision. I was ending a thirty seven year career, leaving so many good friends for the isolation at home. I knew that I would miss the comradery of the Goodyear "family" that I had worked with for so long. But I had no real choice. It was the only solution to a problem that was not going to get any better. The money loss was not an issue, since there would be no special retirement home in

North Carolina, no need for vacation money to see the world, and probably only one person to support in the foreseeable future. I now had only one mission - take the best possible care of Patty in the time that she had left.

So it was that on one particular afternoon, when I was already mentally slowing down and easily distracted from work, larger life issues captured my attention. For reasons unknown to me now, I felt the need that day to cover much of my life philosophy in this one letter to our children. I wonder if I might have been concerned about the length of my own life, as I had been some months before, and needed to impart my perceived wisdom while I had the chance. Maybe I felt that, although we talked often I just hadn't told them enough about me and how I felt about them. Maybe I was just scared that I hadn't done enough for them. Whatever the reason the message was important to me then and it is shared as an indication of where I was at that particular time.

To: Cathy, Doug & Laura

July 22, 1995

From: Ron Gries (known to you as 'Dad')

Subject : Friday Afternoon Ramblings

It's been a while since I gave you any of my philosophical ramblings. I'm pretty much bored with work this afternoon and it's too hot to do anything outside, so I thought this might be a good time. I have been doing a lot of thinking recently on the meaning of life and how best we earthlings can come to grips with it. So I thought I would share some ideas with you and, of course, offer some advice gleaned from 59 1/2 years on this particular planet. I like doing it in writing for a couple of reasons. It's easier for me to collect my thoughts as I'm writing and the computer also allows for easy revision. These are not the kind of subjects that come up normally in our conversations. And most important of all, you don't have any pressure to respond now or ever. So with that preamble, here goes.

I would wish for you a very strong faith life and absolute trust in the Creator. There is no way that I can make sense of life. To say that it isn't fair, by our standards, is certainly true. Why should your mother have to suffer so much? Why should your uncle Ray, one of the world's great fathers, have to go way too early? Why did Arthur Ashe, an ambassador of goodwill, get AIDS from an infected needle? What about Oklahoma City? And on and on. I don't have any answers except for faith and hope. There is a plan, although I don't know the details. There is a God who authors the plan. This is a given. And there is a spirit life after this bodily one—and it will be forever—and it will be in the everlasting Light. Yes, I agree this is oversimplification. I don't consider myself a great thinker. But I can tell you one thing for sure. It's been what has sustained me through some difficult times and it will continue to sustain me for as long as I live.

Wow, that was heavy. But it needed to be number one. Now for something a little lighter. And in this area I couldn't be more proud of you. Take good care of the body you were given this time around. It's the only one you're going to get. If you take care of the physical side it will help all aspects of your life. Eat well, whether or not that includes the dreaded meat, Laura. Get enough rest—this is important for active singers. And keep exercising. I think you've got pretty good genes. Your job is to make good use of them.

Did I mention *Daily Word*? Did I tell you that I think it was the single most important thing in helping me through crisis? Did I tell you how quickly it can be read each day if it is in a prominent place? Did I tell you that I will keep providing the subscriptions for you whether you read it or not? Are you ready to throw up? I'm done with this subject.

Money is an interesting subject. I can be brief. Give it all the respect it deserves, no more and no less. We need it to live. It will not bring us the elusive happiness we seek. Happiness doesn't come from "things." It comes from within. And within is not a bank vault. This in no way should influence any gifts you might be considering for me. I said "things" won't produce happiness. I didn't say they wouldn't provide some joy.

Don't let anger ever get the best of you. This doesn't mean you can't be angry. Lord knows there are enough injustices around to be angry about. The secret is to use the anger constructively for change, not letting it consume you. Anger can be very destructive to self if unchecked. I can attest to that.

Friends are important, family is even more important. Both take work to nourish. Put the effort in and you will be rewarded.

If possible find a life's work that you enjoy. You'll be spending a lot of time at it so why not enjoy it. I've been very fortunate in that regard and I wish the same for you. All of you have incredible talents—probably because of your enlightened choice of parents—so use them in a way that brings you satisfaction, and enough money so that you don't have to call home.

Which brings me to "HUMOR," the one word that defines my life better than any other. I don't know why I like to laugh so much. Or why my mind sees humor in almost everything. I'm glad I'm the way I am. I don't know that I would like to be married to someone like me. Your mother should get a special award for putting up with me for so long. But humor is good. I'm sure you are aware of the proven medical benefits from humor. I've always said that God must have a giant sense of humor. You only need to look at His creatures to see that. Are we funny animals or what? Seriously, don't be afraid to laugh at yourself. Chances are you do as many silly things as the people you laugh at so why not have the extra laughs on yourself. It doesn't cost any more.

Well, thank goodness, I'm running out of steam. I don't even know if you are still reading. I only have one more thought and parental directive for you. Take real good care of yourself. Forgive yourself when you need to. Enjoy your successes and accept your failures as part of your growth. End each day with no anger or unfinished business with anyone. And start each day with the idea that it is the first day of the rest of your life and all good things are possible.

As always, I am available at any time to talk about these or any other subjects you might wish to discuss. If you don't feel the need, that's OK too. That's the good thing about the written word. No pressure. Not that parents would ever put any pressure on children! Did we talk about the great sacrament of matrimony? Just kidding.

Mom and I are looking forward to seeing each of you in the coming weeks. Till then be good and take care. Love, Dad

## Alone but With Help from Above and Below

As Patty's condition continued to decline through 1995 and into 1996 she slowly lost much of her strength and eventually became a prisoner of our home, and later of our bedroom. I followed my plan and retired at the end of 1995 to care for her on a full time basis. With help from friends I was able to manage. They would come over three times a week to sit with her for a couple of hours while I went to play the tennis that recharged my mind and body. The rest of the time I was able to take care of the house (with twice a month assistance from a caring professional), shop, cook (it's amazing how much I learned from some very good recipes and instruction from Patty), do the laundry, and take her to the hospital for the necessary monitoring visits and palliative radiation treatments. I was also in charge of keeping track of the multitude of medications for the pain, depression, appetite, diarrhea and insomnia that plagued her. Those were the easy parts of the job, the physical side that I could handle. The hardest part by far was the strain of trying to help her make some sense of the life that was tormenting her.

I believe this would be a good time to report on a major blessing that my God provided especially for me. During the entire time of our struggle I was never sick, not even for one day. It was as if He decided to answer my daily prayer for strength with an unprecedented time of good health. I was tired much of the time, with Patty mostly upstairs requiring a lot of attention and much stair climbing. But I was never ill and very rarely even a little symptomatic. There was not a single day that I couldn't take care of her. It is often said that God works in mysterious ways. I agree.

Throughout her ordeal Patty was well aware of the reaction of her friends to her situation. She had always treated friendships very seriously, seeing them as very important and putting a lot of effort into them. The fact that some did not necessarily treat them so importantly caused her some real pain over the years. Although most of her friends were female, it is still true that her illness, especially when it became terminal and confining, separated "the men from the boys," to use an old expression. At one point she was so distressed by the "friends' that had deserted her that I followed up our conversation with a poem. Much later, when she was gone, I would confront the issue of what to say to those who had deserted her if they came to the funeral. I felt some anger and imagined screaming at them, "Couldn't you have visited, or called, or sent a card telling her that you were thinking of her?" But I decided not to say anything. I wasn't sure it would make a difference to them, Patty no longer needed any help, and I was just too tired to care anymore.

At the other end of the spectrum were the people who rose to the occasion during this time and showed me the depth and power of human love. One who stood out was Jane, who moved me to write.

## ALONE

"Why don't they visit,
          or at least send a card?"
Her words came so softly.
The pain was bad today,
          physically and emotionally.
She was thinking about
          those that she called "friend."
True there was the special group
          who stayed in constant touch,
          providing company, flowers,
          supportive messages and treats,
          always with their love.
But today it was not enough.
The despair was growing
          as the disease
          relentlessly advanced.
Today she needed more
          from the others
          who did not appear to care.
And I suspect that she wondered
          if she was the one
          who had not been
          enough of a friend to them.

Once again I felt helpless
          in the face of her pain.

I tried to remind her
> of how much we were blessed
> with the number who truly cared.
I mentioned that others too
> have problems of their own that,
> while not comparable to hers,
> would still occupy them.
It was not enough, of course.
I knew it wasn't.
How could I ease her mind
> that could still read the signs,
> still wonder about friendship.

After a few moments of silence,
> she said that she was really tired,
> and would like to sleep for awhile.
I turned out the light and closed the door.

## JANE

Her name is simply Jane.
She masquerades as a quiet wife and mother,
> but I know her secret.
She is a guardian angel,
> more particularly, my Patty's guardian
> angel.
When Patty's progressing cancer
> drastically confined her life
> to the four walls of our bedroom,
> she looked to her angel for help.
And, as angels do, Jane responded.
She visited every Monday
> and brought with her an arsenal of
> weapons
> to help fight the life draining disease,
> while I left for a spell to ease my mind
> by thrashing a tennis ball.
Jane brought conversation when Patty was able,
> listening when important things needed
> to be said,
> encouragement always,
> and quiet closeness when energy was low.
I would return to watch Jane leave,
> always with a tender kiss on the forehead
> that said, "you are special,"
> and a heartfelt "I love you."
It is not easy watching a good friend die.

But Jane insisted on coming every week,
>ever though I said I could get others.
Jane told me she too was profiting from the
>experience.
At first I didn't fully understand
>because I knew how hard it was.
But slowly I learned Jane's secret,
>known to guardian angels and special
>people.
The sharing of love enriches all
>givers and receivers alike.
It expands to fill a room,
>a house,
>a city,
>and finally, a world.
It is a lesson for us all,
>and it comes directly
>from a guardian angel named Jane.

## We Do The Best We Can with the Hand We're Dealt

Throughout the long ordeal we did manage to manufacture some opportunities for a little enjoyment. As Patty's mobility and strength diminished we improvised to find some fun. Patty had always liked cards so we began to play gin rummy. While she always claimed to be non competitive she definitely preferred winning to losing (something I had always admitted.) We had bought her a wonderful sound system some years before and it provided much pleasure when she became homebound. We had also bought a video golf game to substitute for the real golf she was so passionate about. The game was so realistic that I found myself enjoying the challenge with her. And of course there were the televised golf and tennis tournaments that we watched together, rooting for our particular favorites. We especially enjoyed tennis tournaments where our favorites played against each other. With cable TV there seemed to be opportunities every week for us to "play" the games she loved. Movie videos were another source of entertainment since we were both avid movie fans. I had to be careful in the selection of movies since so many of them involved serious life and death issues that she did not need to see. Fortunately there was usually an ample supply of mysteries, comedies and love stories that we both enjoyed. Once in a while I made an honest mistake and it caused both of us some pain.

Our main source of pleasure during this time, however, was the network TV programming of drama and sitcoms. We developed a regular nightly schedule of shows that we both enjoyed. And we got very much involved in the character's lives, even as our lives were so limited. I remembered from my childhood how my mother listened regularly o the radio soap operas to pass the time while she was working so hard caring for us. Now we were doing the same, as our TV favorites took the place of the social life that was no longer possible. We became totally involved with our TV friends, watching their lives unfold even as we silently knew where our lives were headed.

Although there were diversions for us within our home, it was sometimes bittersweet. Watching golf on TV and playing the video version could be fun. But they really couldn't take the place of playing, especially for someone who saw the special beauty of the game and the surroundings. As time went on, the advance of the disease and the increasing strength of the medications also affected her enjoyment of TV. She would sometimes drift away from the game or the shows and then could become upset at her lack of concentration. It was sad for me to watch this vibrant person be relentlessly slowed down and, in the later stages, lose interest. But we did the best that we could and there were enough good times to later provide me with some pleasant memories.

## Sharing a Life and a Bed

She was always worried that her nighttime restlessness was depriving me of the sleep I badly needed. She suggested many times that I should sleep in one of the other bedrooms. But I would have none of that. There was only one place for me to sleep and that was next to her, where I had been for thirty four years. I needed to be next to her in case she needed assistance. And I needed to be next to her so that I could remember the good times.

## NIGHTTIME

It is three o'clock in the morning
and our world is quiet.
Sleep has eluded me this night.
My body rests easily in the big bed,
while my mind digests every sound.
I listen to the regular rhythms of the furnace,
the mid winter groans of the house,
and the occasional muted car engine
that always makes me wonder
who it is,
and where they are going.
She sleeps next to me
and her sounds are the ones I notice most.
The cancer has changed her sleep,
robbing her of the deep respite
that so powerfully refreshes.
Her night is fragmented and uncertain.
At times the breathing is deep and regular,
and I am comforted.
But it rarely lasts all night.
She will awaken and stir.
I might hear the rattle of the water cup
if the pain dictates another pill.
Or the slow labored walk to the bathroom,
or to the dresser for fresh pajamas,
if the night sweats have appeared.
I stay quiet.
She will worry if she knows I am not sleeping.

And she has worry enough for both of us.
When she has returned and settled next to me
       the rhythm changes
       and the sound effects begin.
Sometimes they are sweet murmurs,
       as if the disease is miraculously gone,
       and life's pleasures are once again to be
       enjoyed.
Other times there are sharp cries
       and I know that she is frightened,
       that the vision is dark and troubling.
Sometimes she forms anxious words
       that just miss being understood,
       but nonetheless convey the troubles
       of a tortured soul.

But then, just as quickly, she is still.
The body movement slows,
       the breathing quiets
       and becomes regular.
She seems at peace.
I savor the moment.
My mind quiets as she rests.
I think about better days
       and restful nights.
I pray for a miracle.

## Parenting and the Children That Come with it

I have always taken parenting seriously, maybe too seriously. Patty and I made a good set of parents. I was the conservative one, wanting to teach them everything that I thought was important, trying to keep them young longer than they needed to be, worrying excessively. Patty was by far the freer spirit. She wanted them to explore more, test themselves more, follow their own road to the future. That's how she led her life. I think that we were a good pair for them, offering a rich blend of parenting. One thing we agreed on. Our kids would always have our attention and our love. I can proudly say, and I am confident that they would agree, that we did our best work with them.

I have always liked to write, but did little over the years other than occasional poems to Patty for very special occasions. Now her struggle provided me with the introspection that led to many poems. Some of them were written as tutorials as I thought about the complexity of our lives. I would on occasion send them to the kids along with various articles that I, in my parental wisdom, thought might help them along in the frantic world of young adulthood.

The kids themselves are an interesting lot, especially in their individual reactions to the sad situation. They are all successful singles in Chicago. Cathy, the oldest, is a typical oldest child if there is such a thing. She was our learner child and caught all of our mistakes during parenting on-the-job training. But she survived nicely. She is most like me with a very independent nature, industriousness, a practical approach to life and an understanding of the value of friendship. Cathy's support was very evident through the illness as she recognized, much more than ever before, her strong emotional attachment. Doug, our middle child, was more concerned with Patty's struggle than he could ever admit. He's an engineer with a sensitive side that always pleased his mother. They had that special mother-son bond and her illness bothered him more than he could talk about, especially when he visited. Doug is in most ways like Patty and her father, my main contribution being his sense of humor and a love of athletics. Laura, our youngest, was Patty's soul sister, with the gift of sensitivity and the ability to put emotions into words. She was devastated by the sad turn of events, but also determined to provide the much welcome emotional sounding board.

I tried not to interfere with the way the kids handled Patty's illness, recognizing that there is no right or wrong way, as long as the message of their love and support, coming in different ways, was received. For Patty and me it was very clearly received. What I attempted to do with my writing was to put our family's situation into an overall framework of the total life experience as I saw it. I could not make any real sense out of this tragedy. I didn't expect them to do any better. But I did want them to try to find some value from this sad experience, even as I was searching while I was doing the writing.

## ON LIFE

Treat life as a gift from God.
Don't spend too much time being unhappy
    at the tricks life plays on you,
    or at the bad fortune
    you might sometimes encounter.
There is no such thing
    as true equality
    as far as life is concerned,
    except for one major item.
Our Creator gives each of us
    certain special gifts,
    or, in some cases,
    certain special handicaps.
This is not equality.
However, he also gives each of us
    an equal chance at using what we have
    to try and do our best
    to love and praise Him,
    take care of our neighbor,
    and earn eternal life with Him.
This is what life is all about.
It is definitely a struggle,
    but it is also a gift
    which we are given for a time,
    to use as best we can.
There is much goodness and happiness
    to be found in life,
    if we only search it out.

Life can be an adventure of great magnitude
      if we accept it openly
      in the spirit in which it is given,
      and start each day by thanking God
      for creating us,
      and promising Him
      that we will make it worthwhile.

## TRUST

There will be some times
    when your path isn't clear,
    when difficult choices
    fight hard for your ear.

When anxiousness rises
    and life tests you so,
    there's one voice to follow.
Don't worry, you'll know.

It's your very own voice,
    buried deep down inside.
The one you can't fool,
    the one you can't hide.

But first you must quiet
    the noise all around,
    so that you can hear
    your most personal sound.

That voice will then answer
    your most heartfelt plea.
It will show you the path.
Just try it, you'll see.

You won't always like
    what your voice says to you.

Sometimes it will cause you
      a hard thing to do.

But trust what you find
      when you look deep inside.
It comes with His love.
For in you He resides.

## GIFTS

I pretty much take sight for granted.
It must be awful to be blind,
    to not see the flowers of spring,
    the colors of fall,
    the pageantry of football,
    the face of a loved one.

Can you imagine what the deaf miss?
Beethoven, Mozart, Springsteen, Willie Nelson,
    the music of the songbirds,
    the sound of the ocean,
    the laugh of a loved one.

Being paralyzed must be terrible,
    to be unable to run on a sports field,
    or stroll slowly with a lover
    in a flower filled field,
    or across a sandy beach,
    or simply to walk.

I've always eaten well.
I've never been so hungry that I hurt.
I have trouble even comprehending
    the famines of the third world.
Starvation there is real.
It is a horrible way to die.

Freedom is something I take for granted.
What if I were imprisoned in a jail cell,
      or in a country with no freedoms,
      or a city slum with no hope,
      or in a mind that won't function,
      or a crippled body that always hurts?

What if I had no family to share love,
      no friends to support me,
      no faith in God,
      no hope in His love?

My car wouldn't start this morning.
My team lost again last night.
I might need a root canal.
Life really sucks!

## FELLOW TRAVELERS

We are all fellow travelers,
    united in our search
    for the true meaning
    of our uncertain existence.
We meet each other along the way,
    beginning with the mother
    who carries us safely,
    until we are formed
    and emerge through the miracle of birth.
Some we will know and love for a lifetime.
Others will enter for a time
    and then disappear from our lives,
    as circumstances and geography intervene.
Many we will call friends.
Some we will call special friends,
    those who share themselves with us,
    and accept us for who we are,
    supporting, rather than judging,
    knowing how much we need each other.
It makes little difference,
    in the grand scheme of life,
    how many human encounters we have.
What is, however,
    of paramount importance,
    is that we view each encounter
    as a glorious opportunity
    to share with another

61

our joy,
our pain,
our fears,
and our hope,
as we travel together,
searching for the key
to the ultimate mystery
that is God's presence.

## PARENTS

I think I understand
    the unpredictability
    and downright scariness
    of being a young adult,
    because I've been there.
And while the times have certainly changed,
    most of growing up
    is still pretty much the same.
But how would they understand us?
They haven't been parents,
    and there is no other way to learn.
Besides, they are busy enough
    trying to find out who they are,
    and what this crazy world of
    young adulthood
    is really all about.
Growing, learning, experimenting, doubting,
    and simply wondering
    takes all of their energy.
How could they possibly understand
    a parent's love,
    a parent's pride,
    a parent's fears,
    a parent's hopes and dreams for them.
How could they know
    about the nagging question
    just below the surface
    of every good parent's consciousness,

"Did I do enough for them?"
Only when they are blessed with children
      will they truly understand.

Sometimes,
      when I have been particularly meddlesome,
      in that special way reserved for parents
      who care greatly for their children,
      they will say mockingly,
      but, I sense, lovingly,
"Dad, you are SUCH a parent!"
There is only one way I can respond,
"Thank you."

## The Wonder of Marriage

It would be nice if I could report that all of our marriage problems disappeared during this long period when Patty was slipping noticeably. It would be nice if I could report that I always ministered to her unselfishly, taking perfect care of her with a loving smile always on my face. It would be nice if I could report that Patty was ever attentive to her caregiver's needs, even as she was slowly losing her fight. But it wouldn't be the truth. The issues that had divided us over the years, and caused us on more than one occasion to question whether we should stay together, did not miraculously disappear. We still had our disagreements, most of them caused by the differences that separated us. Patty had a brilliant and creative mind, a serious manner, confidence in herself, the will to succeed, a very vocal nature, a memory bank that held prodigious amounts of information, serious anger at the world's mistreatment of women, a vision of a world filled with love, and a genuine need to make the world and me over into her image. I, on the other hand, had a very good mind with the poorest possible memory, much less self confidence, an affable but guarded nature, extreme love of sports as player and spectator, a slightly irreverent manner, a value system that put a premium on humor and fun, and the firm belief that things would be better if she just tried harder to accept the world and me the way we were.

When I think of our marriage now, I see the marvelous complexity that made it at the same time exhilarating and frustrating. I suspect, in looking around at other marriages, that we were no different than others. I marvel at the plan that unites two such different physical and emotional beings for the purpose of furthering the species. I can now see how I needed this particular person I fell hopelessly in love with to bring out parts of me that I never knew existed. It wasn't easy for me or for her. She spent so many years in the traditional role of unquestioning wife and dutiful mother, all the while knowing that at some deep level she had special gifts that were unrealized. It was only after the kids were mostly raised, in the late 70's, that she could return to the school she loved and satisfy her search for knowledge, gaining undergraduate and graduate degrees in Social Work. It was during this time period that her personal growth threatened our marriage. I simply could not compete with her intellectually, and my inability to share myself fully often frustrated her. It didn't help that we both were very strong willed. While she complained that I could not fill all of her needs, I asked her just to accept the good parts of me. To her credit, she did recognize the strength and love I brought to our marriage, even as I recognized her dedication to being the best possible wife and mother. It was not easy for her, loving this seemingly simple but complicated man that she married. Her constant quest for tasting more of life's adventure and fully using her remarkable gifts was in direct contrast to my need for simplicity and order. But whatever our differences, we worked through them, knowing at the deepest level that we truly loved each other.

Long after she died I played an audio tape I found from 1994 when she was consulting with her special angel Simon in an effort to heal herself. The tape summarizes our existence together so beautifully. Out of the blue Simon says, "Your husband is a good man," and visualizes me, laughingly and apologetically, as a "square block of wood." Patty laughs loudly, and quickly agrees with the assessment saying, "I understand completely. I've yet to find the right chisel." Simon then says, "You have to love that square block of wood and accept it for what it is. And just say, 'I love you the way you are,' and don't try to change him." Patty agrees and says, "I've known for a long time that he loves me to his capacity." Simon comments that I do not interrupt the work that Patty is doing, unorthodox though it may be. Patty agrees, saying, "No, he doesn't, and he won't." Simon closes this section by asking Patty to not burden me with too much and mentions that those like her who are supposed to do certain things have been given someone to take care of them. Patty responds, "That's exactly what I believe. That's come to me. He will take care of me without question."

To say that listening to this passage was an emotional experience for me would be a gross understatement. It put into perspective something I knew at a deep level through all the years of our marriage. There was never any question that she loved me and that I loved her. It was as simple as that, although we did our best as humans to complicate it.

As these two unlike spirits searched for the common ground, a new element was added, anger bordering on rage at the uncontrollable cancer in a person who needed to be in control. She had a right to this particular anger. It wasn't directed at a difference of opinion or an insensitive act, or a problem of the world. This was anger directed at the particular and personal disease that put her in this awful place, with hope essentially gone. I happened to be the closest one to her and to this anger. And I caught much of it. Most of the time I could deflect it and keep it in perspective. Once in a while I couldn't and responded in kind. I am not proud of my behavior in those instances. But I know that my reaction was honest, if not appropriate. And I know that her illness had a major impact on me also, even though I was healthy and would survive. It may not be easy to understand, given the conditions, but it was clear to me that I could still be hurt by this person I loved and cared for. Fortunately, we could always repair the damage. And I learned, through some timely spiritual reading, that I could always forgive myself and move on. We hear so much about forgiving others for the hurts they cause. But we need to hear more about recognizing our human frailties and forgiving ourselves. For long term caregivers, who will slip from time to time, this is especially important.

## ANGER

She had a lot of anger,
        and why shouldn't she?
The cancer that was stealing her life
        was not something she deserved.
Why had the doctors
        prescribed massive radiation
        for the acne that haunted her
        through those difficult teen years?
Shouldn't they have known
        that twenty five years later
        her thyroid would be deadly cancerous?
And what about the doctor then,
        who didn't follow up early enough,
        when it might have been stopped?
Then there was the fibromyalgia,
        that few people understood.
The unyielding pain was real.
        and sometimes overpowering,
        with no relief in a bottle,
        or in a needle.
She had a right to her anger,
        and sometimes it would fall on me.
I was the closest to her,
        with children 300 miles away,
        and no family close.
Naturally we had our issues.

Thirty four years of marriage
>will prick  the scabs of hurt,
>as well as stroke the joys of love.
So I was a convenient target.
One day I asked her
>why she didn't take out her wrath
>on her friends who helped me.
She answered with the honesty
>that facing death will promote,
>"Because if I did they would leave,
>and you can't."
She was right of course.
I couldn't, and I didn't,
>and eventually,
>when she became accepting,
>the anger left,
>and the love triumphed.

## Assisted Suicide

No issue had captured the hearts and minds of the Michigan popu-
lation more than the subject of assisted suicide. It is at once a
legal, moral, religious and most personal issue. With Patty's condition deteriorating, the issue was frightening in its closeness to
us. We talked about it on the occasions when the struggle just
seemed too great. Better than most, we understood the anguish
of the terminally ill and the ones who love them. Patty could get
very despondent on occasion, wanting so badly for her ordeal to
be ended. But we both knew without a doubt that, no matter
how terrible her situation, we could not possibly condone the
willful ending of her life. It just didn't fit with the meaningful
spirituality in our lives.

Later on, after she was gone, I attended an open meeting to
discuss the merits of an assisted suicide bill making the rounds in
the Michigan legislature. At that meeting I heard from a number
of groups on both sides of the issue. Most of the remarks had
some merit. But to me the most telling testimony came from three
severely disabled multiple sclerosis patients who, with all of the
strength that they could muster, spoke passionately about their
opposition and the meaningfulness they still saw in their lives. I
was totally struck by their candor and their view of life. I mar-
veled at how they could search through the agony and helplessness of their situation and find the sacred value of every life. I
wish that all families questioning the value of a loved one's diminished life could hear their heartfelt message. It was an emotional evening for me, for I had seen this very issue reflected in
the courageous spirit of the one I loved.

## I DON'T WANT TO LIVE ANYMORE

It was a routine visit
    with her oncologist,
    a kindly soul.
He had no magic cure for her.
There was not even
    a clinical trial
    anywhere in the country
    that could offer any help.
He could only monitor
    the progress of the dread cancer
    as it spread through her bones.
On this particular visit
    she was unusually despondent.
She asked what he could do
    to relieve her suffering.
The struggle had become
    far too difficult.
Even the increasing morphine
    could not stop all of the pain.
The doctor listened patiently
    to her earnest plea.
He repeated his desire
    to help as best he could,
    to make her comfortable.
He knew what she might be thinking,
    although the exact words were never used.
He also knew that he was limited
    in what he could do.

I knew that she wasn't serious.
She was just so sad that day
So we sat there,
      the three of us,
      wishing her ordeal could be ended,
      but knowing that only time
      would accomplish that.
Finally she ran out of energy,
      as the tears formed in her eyes.
The only sound in the room
      was her quiet sobbing.
When the sobbing stopped
      she composed herself,
      we thanked the doctor,
      and we left.

## WHAT WOULD YOU DO?

I would sometimes be asked,
    when a particular situation
    arose for another,
    "What would you do?"
My response was usually quick,
    firm and decisive,
    right to the point.
I prided myself
    on this innate gift
    to bring the wisdom of Solomon
    to these weighty matters.
Such arrogance!
The last three years changed that.
It was the issue
    of assisted suicide
    that first showed me
    how presumptuous I had been,
    and the importance of compassion.
I was firmly opposed.
But when her pain and depression,
    and the certainty of death
    consumed her,
    she wanted so desperately
    to have the final relief.
I found myself wanting it for her,
    although I was still opposed.

Then I thought of other life issues,
    like abortion,
      which I could never condone.
What if my daughter were raped,
    and became pregnant?
And what would I tell my son,
    if his country called on him
    to fight a war that I thought unjust?
How about the death penalty,
    for those who make tragic mistakes?
What if I had the decision,
    and it was someone I loved?

I've changed my response
    to the question,
    "What would you do?"
Now I simply state
    what *I like to think I would do.*
And then I add,
    "But I don't know for sure,
    and won't unless it happens to me."

## The Phone Call

In June of 1996 golf's United States Open was held at Oakland Hills in Birmingham, Michigan, less than fifteen minutes from our home. Patty and I shared a few favorite golfers, including Tom Watson who set the standard for excellent play, sportsmanship, and total respect for the game - a true superstar. As a surprise for Patty I had a note put in Watson's locker the week of the tournament, explaining Patty's condition and prognosis and asking him if he could possibly make time to visit her or call. With the pressures on the man, who would probably be in contention for the championship, it was certainly a long shot. But it didn't hurt to try. As it turned out Watson was indeed in contention on Sunday, but slipped a bit to miss a chance at the title. It had to be very disappointing for him to get so close. Patty and I watched on TV and were also disappointed. About seven o'clock that evening, an hour after the tournament had concluded, and while I was getting a roast out of the oven, the phone rang. I had taken over answering the phone some time before, but this time I couldn't. Patty picked it up and began a conversation. Curious to know who it was, I listened as I fussed in the kitchen. It seemed to me, from her description of her situation, talk about the golf tournament just concluded and some lighthearted banter, that she was talking to an old friend who was catching up on her condition. Soon she was having difficulty talking, and tears formed in her eyes as she thanked the caller and hung up. She turned to me with a teary, glazed look in her eyes and asked, "Do you know who that was?" When I said no she smiled and said, "That was Tom Watson. He was so friendly, supportive, and down to earth. It was just like talking to an old friend."

In the coming months I lost track of how many times Patty told that story. At that stage of her battle there weren't many things that could put a sparkle in her eyes. But the "phone call" could. And in our severely limited world it was so wonderful to see. I wrote to Tom, thanking him for the call, and he responded with a caring note of support.

After Patty died, I wrote to Tom to tell him and again thank him for his kindness. He wrote a wonderful expression of sympathy in return that I will always treasure as a reminder of how much good there is in people, and how even the worst tragedy offers, along with the pain, the opportunity for the honest expression of love.

# Book Two

## *A TIME FOR SAYING GOOD-BYE*

## The Last Six Months

In August of 1996, it was clear that Patty's earth time was drawing to a close. She had been through so much for such a long time that her mind and her body were both worn out. It was time to begin the countdown to the better life promised by the God that she truly believed in.

I did not do much writing those last six months. I don't know why. There were so many ideas running through my head. But I guess seeing her through the last part of our long life together just took all of the remaining energy that I had. However, I did later recall with clarity a number of important events and ideas from that time period and was able to write about them. It's amazing how some events are so indelibly inscribed in the mind that they are relived with all of the attendant emotion when something triggers them.

The final poem in this group, 'I'm Not Ready," was written in the wee hours of the morning of February 15, 1997 after a long vigil at her bedside. She died three days later.

## MORPHINE AND MIND

The march of the morphine
    was inevitable,
    as the pain increased.
First came the pills,
    so small but so powerful.
Then the patches,
    in increasing strengths.
Finally, the IV drip,
    when nothing else
    would stop the pain.
The morphine worked
    for the most part
    at controlling the pain.
But what a price to pay
    for a woman
    so mentally gifted.
It was so sad to see,
    the gradual lessening
    of that brilliant concentration.
First came the difficulty
    with her monthly budget,
    when the numbers
    just wouldn't add up.
She was so proud of that budget,
    and then she had to let it go.
Then came the confusion
    with her medications,
    which she wanted to control.

Finally, even the TV
    became an irritant
    when she couldn't concentrate
    on her favorite programs.
It was so sad to watch
    a powerful mind
    slowly lose its power
    to the necessary drugs.
I know how sad it was for me.
I can't even imagine
    how horrible it must have been
    for one so gifted,
    so sure of herself,
    so enlightened.

## MIRACLES

When her time on earth
  was clearly numbered in weeks,
  and the long suffering
  seemed about to end,
  curious things happened.
A strange calm came over her
  as her spirits rose.
Her morphine dulled mind
  regained its wondrous clarity,
  and she actually gained strength
  with no real reason for it.
She thought briefly of recovery
  and in a quiet moment together
  asked if I believed in miracles.
I said that I most certainly did,
  although I had never witnessed one.
She smiled,
  as if she knew something I didn't.

There would be no miracle
  to save her life.
She died a few weeks later.
But maybe that special time
  really was a miracle of sorts,
  when her pain eased,
  her mind sharpened,
  and fear of death left her,

replaced by a calm acceptance
of her coming trip to eternity.
Maybe this was a miracle,
orchestrated by a loving God
waiting to welcome
a cherished soul.

## THE LAST "I LOVE YOU"

Her last words to me were "I love you,"
　　on the night she thought
　　the angels would come.
It would be another week
　　before God called her name,
　　but full consciousness would not return
　　and there would be no more words
　　that I could understand.
That last "I love you"
　　was one of untold thousands
　　exchanged over 37 years
　　of courtship and marriage.
Some were said routinely,
　　along with "happy birthday," or "goodnight."
Others carried the depth of feeling
　　that comes at certain times
　　and makes marriage special.
But there were also times
　　when "I love you" wasn't said,
　　when troubles arose
　　that tested us
　　and made us question
　　whether we belonged together.
I'm sure we were no different
　　than other couples,
　　trying to make sense
　　out of an imperfect world

and two very different beings.
But the words would always return,
     along with the feelings
     that kept us together for a lifetime.
I have no memory of the very first time
     she told me that she loved me.
It was a long time ago
     and it's not important.
Only the last time
     need be remembered,
     when she knew our life together
     was soon to end,
     and she left me
     with the "I love you"
     that I will never forget.

## OUT OF AFRICA

It was her favorite movie,
   and she was quite a movie fan.
*Out of Africa* was very special,
   a love story first,
   a tragedy,
   but most importantly,
   a story of strong people
   who felt things deeply,
   and knew the power of love.
The music fit the story
   as well as any music ever has.
It was tender when it needed to be,
   and so powerful at times,
   especially when the plane
   carrying the lovers
   circled over the magnificent land.
It was during those moments
   that a viewer in love
   had to feel how wonderful it was,
   while the one with no special love
   must surely have wished for one.

During her last days,
   when the irreversible coma
   made communication one way,
   she would sometimes be fitful.

I wondered if she was still feeling
      the pain that was so much a part
      of the last years.
The nurse thought not,
      that it was only the restlessness
      of one waiting for final relief.
Talking and stroking did no good,
      so I resorted to the music she loved
      from *Out of Africa.*
It seemed to calm her,
      as if she could picture herself
      soaring with the angels
      over the most picturesque landscape.
I played it many times for her
      in those last days.
And as I listened,
      I soared with her.

## I'M NOT READY

She's going to die soon
    and I'm not ready.

I've had a lot of time
    to get used to the idea.
It's been more than three years
    since her doctor's eyes
    betrayed the hopelessness
    even before he started to speak.
But I'm not ready.

The last two years
    saw the cancer spread
    and the pain increase,
    until she prayed
    for a peaceful death.
I prayed with her,
    but I wasn't really ready.

Last month parts of her brain
    succumbed to disease
    and she weakened,
    until movement was difficult
    and thoughts sometimes confused.
Stronger drugs helped with the pain,
    but she begged God to take her.

I begged with her,
      although I wasn't ready

Now I sit by her side.
I listen to words I can't understand.
I look at her frail body,
      with the visiting nurse's words
      still ringing in my ears,
      "It could come at any moment."
And I'm still not ready.

We had thirty four years together.
Now I tell her I love her,
      I tell her that tonight
      Jesus may come for her
      to welcome her to the eternal reward
      she will surely find.

I smile and hold her hand.
I wonder if it will be tonight
      that the long struggle finally ends.
Whether it's tonight,
      or tomorrow,
      or next week,
I'm not ready.
And I won't ever be ready.

I just don't want her to go.

## She's Gone

She died quietly while I was asleep. It was finally over. The next few days were a blur of necessary activity. I hardly even cried. There were times when my eyes watered, when I couldn't speak due to the lump in my throat. But mostly I was on autopilot, just getting through. There was a certain calmness present as the kids and I completed the arrangements. While we discussed all of the issues openly, they deferred to me for all of the final decisions, fully supporting my choices. I let emotion overrule my usual objectivity in the choice of casket and burial plot. Money was simply not an issue. How could it be when the financial planning that had been so exhaustively done for us to retire comfortably was no longer a factor. Although the hours of the wake seemed to fly by and I have very little memory of individual conversations, I do still clearly remember the viewing room. I had been so worried about her appearance, especially to those who had not seen her for a long time. It was with much apprehension that the kids and I arrived at the funeral home. The room was filled with flowers and I was immediately warmed by the display of affection. I worried about the kids' reaction to seeing her. And I wondered what I would feel. When I saw her I was pleased with what had been done. I had overruled my girls in the selection of her clothes, going for the bold colors that were such a part of her. My girls agreed with me, although they might have seen her differently. Doug was quiet and quickly retreated. He just couldn't bear it. To me she looked at peace and still beautiful, considering what she had been through. I know that "beautiful" is a gross exaggeration. But I wasn't seeing her in the present. I was seeing her in the past. And she was beautiful.

The kids and I selected one of her watercolors to place next to the casket, a vibrant vase of pink peonies. Her talent was evident as the pictures's beauty rivaled that of the real flowers surrounding it. We also had a picture board with forty four pictures chronicling her life from infancy. It was an unexpected time of joy for us, selecting the pictures from a vast collection. The board spoke of her passion for life, her love of family and her quest for knowledge. But to me it mostly said that, though her years were shortened, her life was indeed full.

The church service was both sad and joyous, an unlikely combination. I mourned for my personal loss but was comforted by the church setting and ceremony that reinforced the meaning of a life well lived. I derive much comfort from being in church. I feel closer to my God. And it was never more evident than when we gathered there to say goodby to Patty's earthly life with us, even as we rejoiced in her eternal.

My family is fortunate to number a priest among us. Roger is my cousin and he officiates at all of our family events. Since he knew Patty so well he was able to bring out in his remarks the joy of a life well lived. His profound words were so very welcome in the midst of our sadness.

There are vivid memories I retain of the first night I spent alone after the kids left to resume their lives, memories of being alone and of being afraid of the future. Patty had been much more than a wife to me. She had been a fortress of strength. She had so much knowledge and so much competence. She could mend things and help to mend people. She was unafraid and adventuresome. She was all of the things that I wasn't. And I truly wondered how I would survive without her. I recognized that the physical demands on me would be noticeably lessened.

And I knew that I would not have to work again. But how would I fill my days that had been consumed by her care for so very long? Would the joys that I still knew stay with me in my aloneness. Or was part of the joy just knowing that she was always there with me? Would the grief that I had seen in others overwhelm me after the initial shock disappeared? My sleep was troubled that night as the emptiness of the house and the emptiness of my bed troubled me.

## "I THINK SHE'S GONE"

The words were so soft,
    spoken by my youngest,
    who had spent
    the last days
    keeping vigil with me.
We were taking turns
    at the bedside
    where our Patty
    lay deep in coma,
    waiting for the end
    of her mortal life.
    and the beginning
    of her eternal one.
Laura's simple words,
    which roused me
    from troubled sleep,
    said so much.
We had prayed
    for a peaceful end
    and our prayers
    had been answered.
It was over.

We didn't cry
    as we kissed her
    for the last time.

She was still warm,
      she was at peace,
      and we knew
      that she was safely home.
It was very quiet
      as we stood by her.
What do you say
      when a great ordeal
      has been ended,
      and the sadness of loss
      mingles with the joy
      of salvation?
Nothing needed to be said.
Her life had said it all.

## I'M ALL ALONE

She's gone.
We celebrated her life,
    family and friends,
    knowing she was already
    enjoying her eternal reward.
The children have gone
    back to Chicago,
    where their lives are.
They would have stayed longer
    but I said no.
I had to begin the rest of my life,
    and I wanted to get started.
The last few days
    have been mostly a fog
    that I have had trouble penetrating.
I don't feel the real sadness yet.
Maybe I'm just so tired
    that I can't yet focus
    on how much I've lost.
Maybe I'm just so relieved
    that her ordeal is finally over.
If there is one thing that I do feel,
    it is fear.
I am alone now,
    totally alone.
The life decisions
    that have been shared

for thirty four years,
will now be mine alone to make.
I am not decisive.
I am the great waffler,
with a mind
that has trouble focusing.
She was my rock.
She just knew things,
and filled in my gaps.
Now this life is suddenly mine alone,
with all of its complexity.
I should not be afraid.
I am really quite capable.
I've demonstrated that caring for her.
I should not be afraid.
I just am.

## PLANS

We made plans together,
>   just four years ago.
I would retire at 62
>   and we would settle in North Carolina.
We would play lots of golf,
>   travel extensively,
>   build our dream home,
>   and live happily ever after.
But all of our plans changed
>   the moment her doctor said, "I'm sorry."
The cancer wasn't new,
>   but it had been contained until then.
Now our plans changed,
>   as the illness slowly advanced.
The dream home plan
>   was the first to go,
>   followed by the golf
>   and, of course, the travel.
I retired early at 60,
>   when she needed more care.
Our plans then involved radiation schedules,
>   doctor's visits, medication changes,
>   diet changes and constant pain control.
The TV became our lifeline to the world
>   when movement became difficult,
>   and the bedroom became her home.

We planned our TV schedule
    around her remaining energy.
Then we planned for hospice care,
    last visits with special friends,
    and finally, her funeral.
Our planning together was now complete.
When well meaning friends sometimes ask,
    "What are your plans?"
I usually reply that I have none,
    but what I really mean is this,
    "I will take the time I need
    to recharge my body
    and heal my spirit,
    one day at a time,
    until I am whole again.
Only then will I start to plan
    for the rest of my life."

# Book Three

## *A TIME FOR GRIEVING AND HOPE*

## Grieving Begins but I Don't Realize It

With the funeral over and the kids back in Chicago I began to reorganize some personal and financial matters that had been neglected. I wasn't really "feeling" my loss at this point. I believe that I was so worn out, and so relieved that Patty's long struggle was over, that there was no room for any other emotion. There had been so many times over the preceding four years when I had agonized over her situation. It was enough for me now that she was at rest, and there was no doubt in my mind that she was with her Creator. I had no feel yet for my own situation and did not even want to think about it. It almost seemed like I was offering myself a vacation from life before I tackled my existence without her. I felt tired a good bit of the time, even though I was sleeping quite well.

When I wasn't attending to the business at hand I spent much time napping or just sitting in my recliner, absorbed in the television programming. Many times I would find myself missing large parts of a TV program, as my mind became totally vacant, while my eyes stayed on the screen. Other times I would turn off the TV and just look out the glass doors, taking in the landscape without any conscious thought or feeling. During these episodes I was just numb to the world.

After a few weeks I decided to tackle the thank you notes to the many who had supported us. There were friends who offered to help, but I decided to write them myself. I ended up writing 164 notes, crying much of the time I was writing. I don't believe those tears were for Patty or for me. I don't recall any real sadness or pain. I only remember thinking about the marvelous support from those who responded with such kindness. I was so taken by their generosity that I needed to tell each and every one of them. Among the cards was one signed by all of the Hospice of Michigan people who had done so much for us during the last three months of the struggle. Another card that got my attention actually arrived after I had completed all of the thank you notes. It was from a close friend of my youngest daughter in Chicago. I had only met her a time or two and I was so touched by her gesture that I wrote a small poem for her as a thank you.

## HOSPICE

I can tell you about hospice
      in a very few words.
I don't know how we would have endured
      the last months without them.
The decision was of course hers.
After all
      she was the one who was dying.
There was resistance for a time,
      even though she knew it was inevitable.
For was it not an admission
      that hope was mostly gone?
Wasn't it like a death certificate
      lacking an official date?
Yes, it might have been,
      but it was so much more,
      and it took no time at all
      for her to realize that.
It meant no more time
      in the dreaded hospital.
It meant a team
      of concerned professionals,
      so skilled in caring for the dying,
      and for the involved family.
There was a nurse
      available at all times
      to control the awful pain.

There was a social worker
    and a spiritual counselor
    to combat the uncertainty and fear
    of the impending transition,
    to assist in resolving
    the difficulties of a lifetime.
There was the home health aide
    to help maintain the personal dignity
    of an extremely proud woman.
Dying can be so difficult.
I am thankful hospice was there.
We never felt alone
    with the struggle.
They shared themselves with us,
    with a special kind of love,
    and helped us find
    the way to her promised land.

## COMFORT

When the cold wind of loss
chills my body whole,
the love of caring friends
warms deeply to my soul.

## Encountering the Magnitude of Loss

It hit me unexpectedly as I drove on the interstate that borders the cemetery on a sunny late April day, two months after we said the final goodby to Patty. I had begun wondering about this grieving process. I didn't seem to be following any script that I had read about. Although I knew that grieving was different for every individual, I still wondered why I didn't feel more naked emotion. I wondered if maybe I had already done my grieving during the last stages of her long ordeal, or if I was just not capable of the deep emotions that would trigger all of the raw feelings of loss.

This was the first time since the funeral that I had used the interstate, from which you can clearly see the area of her grave site next to the statue in the Good Shepherd Garden. I had gone to the cemetery a couple of times by the more direct route. On those occasions I talked to her about her new spirit life with God and how glad I was that she was already enjoying her eternal reward. I told her, of course, that I missed her, But I did not cry.

That first interstate drive-by turned out to be a different story, seizing me with overpowering emotion. It felt like so much stored up pain erupted in that one moment. The tears came uncontrollably and I was shocked by my reaction. It was the very first time that I cried so spontaneously and so desperately. It turned out to be the first of many times that I would cry in the car. I wonder now if that view of the grave site from a distance, located under the protection of the Good Shepherd, brought into focus the entire extent of our life together, her courageous battle with the cancer, the earthly finality of death, the promise of eternity, and the aloneness I felt in my car. Whatever the reasons for this experience, I knew two things - I had to rush home and write, and I now had begun to really grieve.

## I SAW HER TODAY

I saw her from the highway today
    in the Good Shepherd Garden,
    under the maple's protection,
    with the beautiful birch
    keeping her company.
Before I even realized it,
    I had said "Hi sweetie" aloud.
Then the tears erupted,
    and the memories overcame me.
It's only been eight weeks apart
    after thirty four years together.
The wound is still fresh,
    and deep,
    and painful.
I picked her final resting place
    so that I could easily find it
    from the often used highway,
    to help me keep in touch
    with a freed spirit,
    at home with her Creator.

I know that time heals,
    that new adventure awaits me,
    that life is still good,
    although lessened somewhat.
So I'll continue to use the highway.

I'll say again, "Hi sweetie,"
      knowing that tears may follow,
      but secure in my belief
      that we are still connected,
      spirit to spirit,
      under the watchful eye
      of the Good Shepherd.

## Remembering the Good

The shock of the cemetery drive-by must have loosened up my store of good memories. For the next four months I would often have vivid flashbacks of our life together and how much she enhanced my existence. These episodes could be triggered in many different ways. It was a special watercolor found while rummaging about, a tennis match on TV, the flowers she so lovingly planted, a bird's beautiful song or something as simple as seeing a couple holding hands. These memories were so life-like that I would become totally immersed in them. On many occasions these experiences would lead to words that tumbled around in my mind until they were formed into ideas capturing the moment. All that I had to do then was find paper and pencil, or a friendly computer keyboard, and let them out.

The tears first loosed during the cemetery drive- by continued as I recorded these moments. But these tears were bittersweet, with some good memories tempering the pain of loss.

## MY PARTNER

When the flowers made their entrance in
    the spring,
    you couldn't help but notice them.
The colors would catch your eye,
    even before the fragrance
    made its presence known.
I had trouble naming them,
    no matter how hard I tried.
But she could name them
    and tell me about their lives.
She loved flowers,
    and they loved her.

Sometimes the different birds would seem
    to compete
    to send their call to my ear.
The resulting din
    was beautiful and dissonant
    at the same time.
She could sort it out,
    without seeing the shapes
    and colors that I needed.
I think they performed best for her,
    because they knew her personally.

If we were in a new place,
  and wandered off the marked trail
  in search of the unlisted adventure,
  I would soon be lost
  as if in a maze,
  with many choices but only one solution.
But she would be calm,
  remembering each turn
  by some tiny feature
  that escaped my mind's storage.

I will still enjoy the sight and fragrance
  of the flowers,
  the beauty and song of the birds,
  and the new adventures.
But it won't ever be the same,
  without my personal guide
  who shared and enriched my life.

## LEGACY

The tulips are so beautiful,
    they've never been so bright,
    the reds and yellows in full array
    reflect the sun's pure light.
She planted them with loving care
    so we wouldn't be alone.
And though she's gone they tell the world
    she made our house a home.

Her paintings hang upon these walls,
    they give the rooms a glow.
Flowers done in watercolor
    put on a dazzling show.
She had a gift with hand and brush,
    and loved her painting so.
I wish that she had had more time
    to let her talent grow.

I brought an English garden home,
    from the place I said goodby.
It sits where I can see it well.
I will not let it die.
She was so good with houseplants green.
They thrived and grew so much.
I think they knew she really cared,
    and felt her loving touch.

Her legacy is all around.
It brightens up my life.
I see her everywhere I turn.
I'm proud she was my wife.
Because she used her talent well,
        because she really cared,
        she taught a lesson very true,
        our gifts are to be shared.

## WATERCOLOR

When she sat down to paint
    she left this world for a time
    and entered a better one.
In her mind the images appeared
    of the flowers she loved,
    pure and radiant
    in their majestic simplicity.
The brush in her hand
    was an extension of her soul,
    as it spread the cherished watercolors
    til the canvas came alive
    with a beauty so true
    that you were tempted to move closer
    to pick up the imagined scent.
She was just learning,
    and honing her untapped skill,
    when the curse of illness
    cruelly stole the brush
    from her weakened hand.
I can only wonder
    about the treasures left in her brush
    by the dread disease.
But I do know for certain,
    that with her ordeal ended,
    she is painting once again
    in a far better place,
    bringing to glorious life
    God's magnificent gift of flowers,
    in His presence.

## I ALWAYS KNEW I LOVED HER

She was only eighteen
    when she first caught my eye
    and captured my soul.
For me there has never been another
    and her loss cuts wide and deep.
Through all the years of ups and downs
    I always knew I loved her.
I just didn't know how much.

For almost thirty five years
    we shared each others lives.
Sometimes our separate spirits were as one.
Other times we were light years apart.
But through it all
    there was never any doubt.
    I always knew I loved her.
I just didn't know how much.

Her children were her pride and joy.
She nurtured, scolded and loved.
I watched her teach independence and trust,
    then witnessed her sadness,
        when they grew and took her lessons
    far away.
Through all those growing years,
    I always knew I loved her.
I just didn't know how much.

Her tulips are spectacular
    this first spring that she's gone.
She had a gift for nature's lore,
    that transformed a yard and a house
    into a beautiful, loving home.
As I watched her work her magic,
    I always knew I loved her.
I just didn't know how much.

As I wander through this lonely house,
    sometimes I feel her near.
Each room has a story to tell,
    as it recounts the varied events of
    our lives.
The memories of laughter, joy and sadness
    constantly remind me that
    I always knew I loved her.
I just didn't know how much.

I still sleep in the king size bed,
    that we shared these many years.
I stay on my half and look at the empty side
    that held my life's companion,
    through the good times and the last
    sad days.
To me it's never been more clear.
    I always knew I loved her.
And now I know how much.

## HOLDING HANDS

One of the things I miss the most
    is the simple joy of holding hands.
Her hands were soft and smooth,
    almost delicate.
They fit mine perfectly,
    like a favorite glove.
The best place for holding hands
    was the movie theatre.
The lights would dim
    and the screen would come alive.
We would settle in,
    getting comfortable,
    anticipation high.
Somewhere along the line,
    one of us would reach over,
    and it didn't matter who.
Our hands would find their mate
    and relax totally
    in that old familiar touch,
    with the occasional gentle squeeze
    to reinforce the closeness
    felt in that private darkness,
    saying without words,
    "We are two today
    but we are also one,
    and I would be here with no other."

Since she's gone I don't often go
    to the movies we loved so much.
The stories and the images on the big screen
    are as good as ever.
But when the lights go out
    and the quiet anticipation sets in,
    there is no loving hand to hold,
    and the theatre becomes a lonely place.

## WIMBLEDON

I watched the tennis from Wimbledon today,
    from England, live on the telly.
They call it "Breakfast at Wimbledon,"
    Saturday and Sunday at 9:00 am,
    Ladies and Gentlemen's finals.
I've been enjoying this show
    for the last twenty five years.
This year produced exceptional tennis
    on the rare sunny days
    when all of England
    praises the weather gods.
But for me this year was different.
I watched alone for the first time,
    enjoying the great tennis,
    but missing my doubles partner
    who shared my tennis world
    and the rest of my life.
She was a good player.
We were a pretty fair team,
    on and off the court.
But we didn't always agree
    about tennis and other things.
I liked the volatile Agassi.
She had her wonderful Petey.
She appreciated the athletic Navratilova,
    I was for the classy Chrissie.

We both liked the gentlemanly Borg
    and couldn't tolerate McEnroe.
The memories are so strong
    on this first anniversary
    of our last Wimbledon together.
I wanted so badly
    for her to share and enjoy it
    one more time with me.
I wanted it mostly for me.
Where she is, every day
    brings even more joy
    than breakfast at Wimbledon.

## WEDDING VOWS

The bride was beautiful,
 in that special way
 reserved for brides.
She wore her mother's dress,
 a reminder of the love
 that led to her existence.
The groom was composed,
 with no nervous signs,
 only a calm assurance
 that he was on the right path.

It was a garden wedding,
 and right next door.
Perhaps it was fitting that the bride
 took those important bridal steps
 down an aisle of grass
 where she had romped and played,
 and grown from infant to adult.

Her father's spirit was present
 in the flower garden he so lovingly
 attended.
Big brother did the escort honors
 while mother looked on,
 no doubt remembering
 when she too walked in that dress,
 down her aisle of dreams.

When it was time for the sacred vows
    I too did some reflecting,
    back some thirty five years,
    when I stood with a beautiful bride
    and promised to love and care for her,
    "for better or worse,
    for richer or poorer,
    in sickness and in health,
    until death do us part."

Our thirty five years of marriage
    saw us experience all that we vowed
    on our very special day.
When death ultimately sent her spirit
    to the final reward with her creator,
    our earthly promises were completed.

My remembrances were so strong
    that I heard little of the actual ceremony,
    as one part of me mourned for my loss,
    while another part wished for the
    new couple
    to hold on steadfast to their vows,
    as long as they draw breath.
For there is no greater gift
    that can ever be exchanged
    by husband and wife,
    than the promise to love and care
    for each other,

"for better or worse,
for richer or poorer,
in sickness and in health,
until death do us part."

## A Shocking Resurgence of Grief

Just as the experience of viewing her grave site from the highway in late April altered my grief, another visit to the cemetery in August would move me to yet another place. This time it was a routine visit on a beautiful sunny day. I only visited on sunny days since there was too much darkness in her loss. As I parked the car and walked across the grass in the Good Shepherd Garden my feelings were mixed, with good memories tempering the sadness. But that changed quickly and dramatically when I approached the site under the tree and saw the granite and bronze marker for the first time. It had been ordered many weeks before with no promise date for the installation. I was totally devastated and felt more alone than at any point in my life. Something about seeing the marker brought home so powerfully that she was really gone and would not return. I cried uncontrollably and could not feel anything except how utterly alone I was.

## CHISELED IN STONE

I went to the cemetery today
    and saw her grave marker
    for the very first time.
The tears came quickly,
    as a thousand memories
    flooded my mind.
All of a sudden it seemed so final.
Perhaps on earlier visits
    the unmarked earth
    did not fully register
    how final my loss.
Perhaps some part of me did not accept
    that she was really gone
    and would not return.
But on this visit,
    the newly installed granite and bronze
    spoke so loudly to me;
    *Patricia A. Gries*
    *April 10,1941 - February 18, 1997*
    *Rest in Peace.*
When I read the marker
    so cold against the ground,
    my loneliness surrounded me
    and I recalled the words
    of an old country song,
    "You don't know lonely
    till it's chiseled in stone."

## The Miracle Rose

My traumatic experience at the cemetery did include an astounding happening that reinforced the magnificence of the divine plan. In the midst of my uncontrolled sobbing I noticed a bud vase with a single fresh rose positioned next to the bronze of her grave marker. There was no indication of a grave nearby. The rose could only belong to Patty, and it matched the bronze roses that I had chosen to surround her name. She had always loved flowers and roses were her favorite. During better times I used to surprise her once in a while with roses, on days when flowers were not expected. It always brought joy to her. During the last year of her life, special friends Hal and Bev kept Patty's bedroom in fresh roses. Hal's hobby is growing roses and I believe Patty got his entire output that year. The roses helped to brighten up a room that was often dark, and once again spoke to the power of love.

A day or so later I talked with Bev and Hal about my experience at the cemetery. They had asked me previously to let them know when they could take some roses to the cemetery, after the marker was placed. I wondered if they had seen it somehow and reacted. But they hadn't. I probably could have done some investigating at the cemetery. Maybe the rose was part of the installation. Maybe it belonged to an unmarked grave nearby. There could be an answer if I persevered. But I decided not to. If you remember back some pages to a poem called, "Miracles" you'll recall that I told Patty that I believed in them but had never seen one. Well, now I had. The rose told me that all was well with her. And that was good enough for me.

## Tears and so Much More

I now was confronted with a chaotic period of conflicting emotions. I would, over the next six months, feel more emotional pain, more enlightenment, and more comfort than I could possibly have imagined. And the mood swings could be absolutely frightening in their severity and unpredictability. I now can see that during that time period I was gradually healing, with good visions slowly replacing the troubling ones. It didn't actually dawn on me until I noticed that my writing was bringing out more traces of hope amidst the grief.

The various stages of grief that I describe were not exact time lines like the months of the year or the duration of a school semester. Rather, they were loose periods triggered by specific events, but overlapping in emotional content. For me the healing process followed the path I have described, and continues to this day, with the good memories and faith in her salvation gradually taking command of the pain. Others will most certainly feel things differently at different times. But I do feel confident that all of us who grieve can eventually find the healing and a future that offers promise. We will take different paths to that future. But if we let the process unfold in all of its mystery, absorb fully all of the emotions that flood our consciousness, accept the help offered, and truly believe in the Higher Power and plan, then we can surely emerge from the darkness and see the light.

## TEARS

They come often and unpredictably.
I cry when the TV brings pictures
        that vividly show the pain and suffering
        of our uncertain human existence.
I cry when the same screen
        brightens with the glow
        of mankind's good deeds.
It seems like my emotions are so close
        to the surface of my being
        that good or bad can trigger the flood.
I didn't used to cry much,
        at funerals of loved ones and friends
        mostly.
Other times my eyes would mist
        and my throat turn lumpy,
        but the real tears were not allowed.
Maybe I was so absorbed with life
        that I didn't fully understand
        how fragile it really is,
        and how important we are to each other.
Maybe I learned too well
        that "big boys don't cry."
Maybe I just never missed anyone
        as much as I miss her.
It always bothered her
        that I didn't cry enough.

It is ironic that her suffering and death
    were the catalysts
    that finally loosened my tears.
Now, when the tears flow,
    I picture her in her eternal home,
    with that special knowing smile,
    and a slight nod to the Almighty.

## WELCOMING DARKNESS

It would probably
    not be surprising
    to those who have experienced grief,
    if I told them
    how I sometimes welcome
    a gloomy overcast day.
It is of course
    a mighty contradiction,
    to the accepted position
    that the balm of sunshine
    will certainly take away
    some of the dark pain.
But there are some times
    when the pain is so great
    that I need to feel my loss
    as deeply as I can,
    if I am to go through it
    to the better place
    that I know awaits me.
It is during these times
    that the sun is an intrusion
    in my dark reverie.
I don't want brightness.
I don't want joy.
I don't want cheeriness.

I want the day
>> to reflect my dark mood
>> so that I can face my grief
>> and feel its magnitude
>> at the very core of my being.

It is only then,
>> at the absolute bottom,
>> that I can truly know
>> that I will survive this trial
>> and be renewed.

When this brief sojourn ends,
>> as I know it will,
>> I will once again
>> welcome the light
>> and let it draw me upward
>> into a bright new day
>> of renewed hope.

## SOMETIMES GRIEF

Sometimes, out of nowhere,
    the grief washes over me
    like the ocean tide
    covers the small stones
    on the sandy beach.
A thousand memories of her
    fight for recognition
    as my mind becomes
    a movie projector gone mad.
The tears flood my face.
I am totally oblivious
    to space and time.
All that I can feel,
    all that I am able to contain
    in that particular moment,
    is that she is gone,
    and that I am alone,
    utterly and completely alone.
I allow myself to sink
    into that moment,
    feeling it with everything I have.
I know I must do this,
    and I also know
    that the moment will pass,
    and it always does.
The tears dry up.

My eyes are again open
　　to the world around me.
A familiar sight or sound,
　　perhaps a bird at the feeder,
　　or a neighbor
　　eyed through the window,
　　reminds me that life goes on,
　　that I have survived,
　　that this world still offers me
　　its wonder and magic.
I am not yet whole.
I am changed forever.
But life is still good
　　if I want it to be.
And I do.

## DIFFICULT TIMES

It has been many months
> since my partnership with Patty
> was interrupted by her journey
> to a much better place.
While I am not alone,
> feeling her spirit
> in the good memories,
> and blessed with much support,
> I am at times lonely.
I know it is to be expected,
> and that helps,
> but only a little.
There are two times each day
> when I am most vulnerable,
> when I go to sleep,
> and when I wake up.
I continue to sleep in the big bed,
> still only on my side.
My bed was shared with her
> for almost thirty five years,
> and in my lifetime
> I never once shared a bed
> with any other.
Even when our differences
> caused silence in the big bed,
> it was better than now,
> for I always knew

that the bad times were temporary.
I am lucky in one respect,
    I usually fall asleep quickly.
The waking is a different story.
Sometimes I will lie awake,
    thinking about another day alone.
Even with a full agenda
    of pleasant work or play,
    it is still sometimes difficult
    to make sense of arising alone.
But I always do,
    and in a short while I feel better,
    and remember that I am commanded
    to do much more with my life,
    until I am called
    to join my Patty.

## ENORMITY

Sometimes,
>  when I least expect it,
>  the enormity of her suffering
>  totally grips me.

For a brief time
>  I am lost in it,
>  the rest of the world
>  suddenly forgotten.

All I can think of
>  is how much she suffered,
>  physically and mentally,
>  for so many years

I wish I could understand
>  why it had to be like that.

I'm no better
>  at understanding now
>  then I was
>  during those long years.

I have no idea
>  how she endured.

I don't know anyone
>  who paid such a price.

And a part of me
>  will always wonder
>  if I did enough for her.

But the larger part of me
    understands better now
    that the plan for us
    will always be
    the ultimate mystery.
I need no longer
    wonder about
    a time of struggle
    that is now long past.
It is better if I
    think of her now,
    in her honored place
    close to her God,
    in perfect joy,
    forevermore.
I can do this
    if I try.

## HEALING

I had been doing better
    I thought,
    until the TV police drama
    took an unexpected turn
    and a policeman's wife
    was asleep in a casket,
    surrounded by flowers,
    with him the lone mourner.
This particular day had been a good one,
    a leisurely breakfast with the paper,
    a lot of welcome sunshine,
    a great visit with a good neighbor,
    my favorite grilled salmon for dinner,
    and some interesting TV,
    until the police drama rudely
    reminded me
    that only eight months ago
    I was the mourner
    and she slept among the flowers.
The tears came so quickly
    from a place deep inside
    that I was surprised.
I didn't try to stop them.
I let them run their course.
And then I was fine,
    able to enjoy the rest of the show.
Maybe I'm slowly healing.
Maybe my life is returning.

141

Maybe the bad times will lessen.
Maybe I just need more time.
And since she's gone,
          time is what I have.

## MAILCALL

I find myself waiting now
    for the afternoon mail.
Since she's gone
    I need that daily contact.
I need to know
    that others care
    enough to write.
It wasn't like this before,
    but then, nothing was the same.
I was not beholden
    to a mailbox
    for a part of my life.
Now I send out my poems
    to the good people
    that I know.
I want to share myself
    with them
    during a difficult time.
But I sometimes wonder
    If mostly I am looking
    for a response
    that tells me
    I have reached them,
    and that my life
    still has a purpose.
She was my purpose
    for so very long,

first through the good days,
when we had each other,
and three special lives
to help form,
then through the tough years,
which left their mark on me.
Now the special lives
are wonderfully developed,
and her spirit exults,
while I wait for the mail
to bring me news
that I am still
an important part
of something good,
and that, most of all,
I am not alone.

## People Who Have Walked with Me

I have always been blessed with good friends. But I suspect that on occasion I took their friendship for granted. It was not something that needed a lot of work, like the relationships with wife and children. How misguided I was! During my grieving I had strong support, which was important since I had no family in the state. But there was a difference now. For some of these folks were still grieving for a lost spouse and others had very serious problems of their own that I had not paid enough attention to. Now I saw more than what they were giving to me. Now I saw their struggle much more clearly and could relate to it in a whole new way. Some of them were heroic people who had been dealt a bad hand by life, as my Patty had. I began to offer them comfort, even as they were consoling me. This was totally new for me. I think that I had mostly left that sort of thing for Patty to do. It wasn't a "guy" thing. Now I didn't have Patty, and wanted to help. So I had to do it myself.

In this section you will briefly meet a few of those who I thought about and wrote about during this stage of my grieving. There is Nancy, the hospice home health aide, who made such a difference with Patty, Adrienne, the daughter of long time friends, who battles multiple sclerosis, and Dolores, an old friend who fights Parkinson's disease. You'll meet octogenarians Ruthie and Charles, friends from better days who re-entered my life when I needed them, and Mike, God's special gift to me, who knows all there is to know about listening and caring. He is also the husband of Jane, Patty's weekly visitor whom you met earlier.

It was Mike who provided the inspiration for the last poem in this group, "Hello Dear Friend," which is a plea to all who are friends with one who is grieving and aren't sure what they should do to help.

## PRETTY LADY

Nancy called my Patty "Pretty Lady"
    and she was right on both counts.
For Patty was indeed still pretty,
    even though the terrible disease
    had ravaged her body.
And there was never any question
    about her being a lady.
She had an air of class about her
    that was noticed the first time you
    met her.
Once she told me that she had been
    a member of royalty
    in one of her earlier lives.
She may very well have been right.

Nancy was part of the hospice team.
She came three times a week
    and I know that she was sent by God
    to care for a proud woman
    during her last months.
It was still important for Patty
    to take good care of her body,
    and look her best,
    under conditions where a less
    proud woman
    might have given up.

I had done my best,
>but I simply lacked the special touch
>that Nancy brought to us.

She faced a difficult task.

The weakness of Patty's body,
>and the hopelessness of her future
>only amplified her need
>for the most attentive care.

For, after all, she had once been royalty.

But there was no need for worry.

From the first, Nancy was up to the task.

She knew her craft well,
>and learned quickly to handle the
>challenge.

The result was brightness,
>and it was so badly needed
>during an otherwise dark time.

I think about Nancy,
>and those like her,
>who have the most important task
>of ministering to the dying
>at a time when personal dignity
>is so very important.

Nancy is called a Home Health Aide.

I think a better title would be "Angel,"
>for that is exactly what she is,
>sent from above to comfort and soothe.

I only hope that Nancy fully understands
>the importance of her work

and the gratitude of the families she
serves.
I suspect she will not get rich
from her efforts.
But what better way
to secure your own place in eternity,
than by helping those who are so close
to making that final trip.

Nancy called my Patty "Pretty Lady"
and that I will never forget.

## ADRIENNE

Her name is Adrienne,
and she is special.
Fate has played
the cruel trick of MS
on her still young body.
It weakens her,
and makes life very tenuous.
But there is no quit in her.
The spirit is alive and well
and cannot be contained.
It emerges through her eyes
that can still sparkle,
and a warm smile
that brightens a whole room.

I had never met Adrienne
until last week.
But on that first visit
I felt close to her.
We hugged and it felt good.
When I left she thanked me
for coming to visit.
But she had it all wrong.
I really owe her the thanks.
By allowing me to share
in the smallest portion
of her great struggle,

she gave me a gift of her spirit
and enriched my life.

Her name is Adrienne,
and she is very special.

## THE SOLDIER AND THE SAINT

Ruthie has always called him Charles.
Chuck simply wouldn't do for the "Colonel."
He is a proud veteran
    who served his country well.
And at eighty years of age
    he still carries himself with authority
    and no doubt would quickly join the fray
    if his country were ever threatened.
But there is also a soft side to him
    that he tries his best to hide.
He feels his faith deeply,
    contributing his time to church and
    community.
That softness extends to his hands
    that craft blocks of wood into delicate ducks,
    so lifelike they would probably swim away
    if placed in a stream.
Chuck is an accomplished man,
    given to sharing his many triumphs,
    and he has much to be proud of.
He can, of course, be cantankerous,
    the curse of the overly bright and talented.
He has always set the bar quite high
    when measuring his own and others' deeds.
I wonder sometimes
    if he fully appreciates those of us
    who are not quite as accomplished.
I believe Chuck is most comfortable

in his military role,
totally in charge,
always in command,
and that is all right with me.
He has earned my respect
and my love,
and I know that he cares about me.

And what of Ruthie the saint?
She qualifies easily for that lofty title.
For hasn't she spent fifty six years
married to military ideals,
holding her family together early on,
when her Charles went off to war,
not to return for more than three years,
to greet the unborn child he had
to leave.
Ruthie is diminutive in stature,
most of her composed simply
of bright loving eyes
and a giant heart.
Do not however, mistake her size for
weakness.
There is a lot of strength here.
It is different than her Charles' kind.
Ruthie's strength is quiet and unassuming,
almost deferential.
But I know her secret.
I know how she raised her family,
and tamed the military.

I can see the love,
> the teaching of christian lessons,
> the example of hard work,
> the bonding of spirit,
> flowing from her to them.

Even now, when others her age would rest,
> she reaches out with her Charles,
> to family, church and community,
> always giving,
> always, I suspect, quietly.

When Ruthie hugs me,
> with all of the strength she can muster,
> and tells me that she loves me,
> I feel a part of something divinely good.

After all,
> isn't that what saints do?


When we gathered
> to celebrate my Patty's life,
> and speed her on her eternal journey,
> Charles and Ruthie were there.

They came fifty miles in a driving rain,
> to honor her and comfort me.

Can you define special people any more clearly?
Can you find a better example of pure love?
I don't think so.
And I was the lucky one
> to receive so much
> from the soldier and the saint.

## DOLORES

Her name is Dolores
  and she is one of God's special people.
She has been dealt
  the cruel blow of Parkinson's.
It weakens her body
  and makes life very difficult.
But the most important part of her,
  her spirit,
  will not be denied.
She simply won't allow it.
Life still holds meaning for her.
She has things she wants to do.
And for her
  disease is just an inconvenience.
She still smiles
  with a genuine warmth
  that enfolds all of those around her.
When she hugs,
  it is as enthusiastic as ever,
  letting the lucky receiver know
  that she cares about them.
That is what makes her so special.
She will not give in to fate.
I know that she must sometimes
  feel so alone in her struggle.
I would only hope
  that she understands

how all of us are connected,
how we all exist
in His love and in His presence,
so that she is not alone.
In fact, it is in her struggle
that we are all inspired,
and mankind itself is elevated.
I hope she understands
how important she is to us,
and how much we care.

## MIKE

His name is Mike,
     not to be confused with Michael.
"Michael" seems too unbalanced,
     too many syllables, too formal.
"Mike" is direct, solid, dependable.
The very saying of it suggests
     strength, purpose, resolve.
And that fits the man perfectly.
When my Patty died,
     and life lost much of its joy,
     Mike responded with that rare combination
     of male sensitivity and action,
     so foreign to our particular breed.
Mike immediately took charge,
     beginning with the offer to host
     the important funeral luncheon,
     providing the warmth of his home
     at such an important time.
Since then he is constantly in touch,
     offering lunches, dinners, golf.
     and, most importantly, listening.
I tell him everything,
     because I know he truly cares.
When I am with him I feel special and loved.
What greater accolade can be given.
My Patty recognized that quality in Mike,
     when we were neighbors years ago.

She wanted me to be more like him,
  but I still had that lesson to learn.
And now, Patty would be happy to know,
  I am learning.
Sometimes we unknowingly teach our sons
  the wrong lessons.
We teach them to be tough,
  to watch out for themselves in an
  impersonal world,
  to not let their emotions get the better
  of them,
  and, most certainly, to be strong and
  not cry.
I'm glad Mike learned different lessons.
I'm glad he cares so much.
I am blessed to be counted among his friends.

## HELLO DEAR FRIEND

Hello, dear friend.
I am so happy to have your company today
    during this difficult time of grieving.
I need your support and your love.
I need to share myself with you,
    along with the memories of her
I hope that you will not be troubled
    if I tell you that this particular day
    is filled with sadness for me.
I hope you don't mind
    if I mention some part of her life
    that is vivid in my mind
    and heavy in my heart.
I wish that everyday I could tell you
    that I was well and strong,
    and brimming with life.
But today I am not,
    and I will not try to fool you.
Rather, I hope that you will understand
    where I am and why I need to be there.
I do not need you to fix me.
Only time will accomplish that.
I just need you to listen and care about me.
And if you see a tear,
    or hear my voice falter,
    do not be alarmed.

I need to experience fully
the grief that I feel.
And I need to share it
with those who care for me.
Please do not worry about me.
Tomorrow will be a better time,
and someday I will be whole again.
Life will one day
again offer its magic and joy to me.
I can't say exactly when that will be.
I only hope that you will stay the course
until that day comes.

## The Everyday

Along with a heightened awareness of the many people who were a part of my life came new attention to everyday events and occurrences. Again my grief had seemingly opened up new aspects of my existence. Simple things now commanded my interest, leading to new insights. I pondered and put into words ideas that my consciousness might have flirted with, but never really clarified. I observed simple events that crystallized immediately into larger ideas I have no explanation for this phenomenon. It is almost as if the good Lord decided that grieving should not be all bad, that there should be some compensation involved. I believe that it happened to me and is continuing to happen, as I seemingly become reinvented with fresh insights and outlooks.

I suspect that I had to let myself be totally immersed in the sorrow and pain of loss before my spirit could be opened to life's revelations. Not that the pain was by any means gone. It could still jump up at any moment with surprising force. But the frequency and duration were now being diminished as I began to feel that there might still be a life with some joy for me.

In November of 1997 I began volunteering with Hospice of Michigan, an activity that would prove to be immeasurably helpful in my gradual healing. Now I could use some of my energy to comfort and assist other families going through what I had been through. Because of my experience I was much more comfortable facing the dying part of living with understanding and compassion. I could offer assistance to patients and families seeking resolution with dignity, hope and peace. And in offering that help I became more attuned to their struggle and less caught up in my own loneliness. I continue the volunteering to this day.

## MYSTERY

The TV screen brings me a vivid story
    of life, love, passion, sorrow.
My head spins as ideas tumble about.
The story is forgotten as my mind fills
    with life's joy, pain, loss, triumph.
The raw emotions of living
    assault my consciousness.
Why did I not see this before
    as clearly as it presents itself now?
I have felt bits and pieces of it before.
But they seemed mere intrusions
    into a life so occupied with the everyday.
Did it take her long suffering
    and the cold finality of her death
    to rouse me from the everyday,
    so that the power of the very life she lost
    could fill my empty spaces?
Did it take the greatest sorrow of my life
    to bring forth the fullest realization
    of who I am, and where I fit
    in the magnificence of our total
    humanity?
My tears of pain mix with those of joy
    until they become indistinct,
    running freely together in a tide
    that I do not even try to stop.

For the tears cleanse me, nourish me,
    wash away my doubts and my fear,
    leaving me with a soothing calmness.
They remind me that my spirit is united
    with her and with all of humanity,
    past, present and future,
    secure in His perfect love,
    born in each and every one of us,
    from all eternity.

## LEAVES AND LIFE

The leaves were late this fall.
But when they started to come down
    it was in a torrent,
    as if some power commanded them
    to finish their appointed task.
Some spiraled wildly to the ground,
    as if they were protesting
    and trying to return to the tree,
    after their journey had already begun.
Still others slowly floated in wide arcs,
    seeming to enjoy one more quiet
    look around
    at the existence they were leaving,
    while choosing their final resting place.
A few clung tenaciously
    to the branches they called home,
    not yet ready to leave and be forgotten.
The leaves themselves were varied.
Some were golden and majestic,
    having reached their fulfillment
    by supplying life and joy to the world.
Others were torn and wrinkled,
    as if the world had treated them shabbily,
    and they had stayed too long.
A few were still green,
    taken before their time,
    cheated out of a full life.

As I watched I was transfixed,
    seeing my own existence
    and my own mortality
    in the falling leaves.
I wondered for a brief moment,
    how my final trip would be taken.
Will I calmly float, in radiant gold,
    satisfied and accepting?
Will I fall wildly, broken and discolored,
    having outlived any usefulness?
Or will I fight my fate,
    trying to recapture what cannot be?
I hope that when my Fall comes
    I will show the gold of fulfillment,
    floating smoothly and quietly
    to the inevitable end,
    and the just as inevitable beginning.

## MOTHER AND SON

The sermon was not particularly interesting.
My eyes left the priest,
    along with my concentration.
They scanned the congregation
    and settled on a mother and young son.
She appeared to be intent on the sermon.
Her arm was casually draped on the shoulder
    of a boy some eight years of age,
    sitting very close.
He was big for his age, with some baby fat,
    and a round pleasant face topped
    with short hair.
While the mother listened,
    her hand gently stroked the boy's shoulder
    and back,
    never once pausing.
The boys eyes appeared to drift a bit.
His body seemed to accept the stroking
    as if he were used to it.
Eventually, his head slipped some
    and rested on the comforter's shoulder.

As I watched the mother and son
    I thought of how important it is
    that sons have mothers to help them
    with the soft side of life,
    while their fathers teach them,

often misguidedly,
about being a man.
My son was lucky that way.
His mother cared greatly.
She loved him and taught him
that boys and men also need
the stroking born of love.
When he was young he liked it.
Then he had to leave her for a spell,
as the world demanded he become tough.
It just wouldn't do to show a tender side,
although it had never left him.
But he came back to her in her last years.
The hugging and the "I love you"
became easier, and then even natural.
I'm glad for my son and what he had.
I'm happy for the little boy in church.
I hope he knows how lucky he is.

## LONELINESS

I have felt alone
    when surrounded by people.
I have felt connected
    when isolated a continent away,
    in a foreign environment,
    among total strangers,
    speaking a language
    I don't understand.

It is not geography,
    or proximity,
    or similarity,
    or language
    that dictate loneliness
    or invites connectedness.
Because these are not
    matters of the body.
They are matters of the spirit.
And if we truly believe
    in the One
    who connects us all,
    we may feel lonely,
    but we will never be alone.

## CANCER

I tell myself over and over
    that the word shouldn't scare me.
But it does.
I remind myself that my mother,
    who I favor most,
    was never afflicted
    to age eighty eight.
But it makes no difference.
    I still worry.
    I have lost a father,
    a sister and her husband,
    my only brother,
    and now my wife.
Maybe I just don't know
    of enough people
    who have beaten it.
I read about them sometimes,
    but I don't know them.
And the people closest to me,
    the ones I love,
    have not been so fortunate.
It is like fighting
    an unseen enemy
    that lurks in our vicinity,
    just waiting for the chance
    to remind us we are mortal.

The statistics can be encouraging,
>if you read of increased cure rates,
>and better diagnostics.

But it does little good
>when the doctor tells you
>that it has struck again.

Then it tests your belief
>in God's glorious plan,
>which I still subscribe to.

I hope and pray,
>that if I am ever caught up again,
>with a loved one
>or myself,
>I will be strong,
>understanding,
>accepting,
>and filled with faith.

## SOMETIMES I WONDER

Sometimes I wonder.......
If the heavy pain comes to me,
     as it came and stayed with her,
     will I be strong?
Will I bear it
     as well as she did?
I'm not very good with pain,
     even the tiny pain that I've known.
I don't know how she did it,
     for such a long time.
I wonder if I could.

Sometimes I wonder.......
When my days are numbered,
     will my faith be strong?
I told her of my faith
     when she knew she was doomed.
I encouraged her.
I was strong.
I was unwavering.
I was certain
     of her final reward
     with a loving God.
But it was not me
     facing the certain death.
And I wonder.

Sometimes I wonder.......
What is the plan for me?
Do I suffer the loneliness
    for a reason?
Does the pain of her loss
    serve me well
    and make me stronger,
    more aware of life's magic,
    better able to love,
    more tuned to the Spirit?
I hope so.
I think so, but,
    sometimes I wonder.......

## THE NUTHATCH

I watch the lone nuthatch,
    technically the white breasted nuthatch,
    as he explores the trunk
    of my large backyard maple.
He is beautiful,
    with his white breast,
    blue-gray wings,
    white face with black cap,
    and chestnut undertail.
But it is not just his beauty
    that captures my attention.
He is climbing my tree
    UPSIDE DOWN,
    exploring from top to bottom.
He appears so comfortable
    in this unusual position,
    able to maneuver easily,
    looking about casually,
    oblivious to his natural disregard
    for the normal, the safe,
    the familiar of the world.
I want to shout through the glass,
    "How do you do that?"
    "Please show me how."
For I see myself in that nuthatch.
I sometimes feel that my world
    is upside down, just like his.

Nothing is the same anymore,
   since she's gone.
I am hanging on life's tree,
   upside down.
But, unlike the nuthatch,
      I am not secure,
      I am not comfortable,
      I do not see clearly.
There are times when I feel
      that I have lost my grip.
      that I must surely fall off.
But then I watch the nuthatch
It rights itself to feed.
It flies away like other birds.
I say to myself,
      "I will do that someday."

## Isn't It Just a Car?

Why would anyone have a section composed of only one poem about a car? The answer is simple. The poem is not about a car. It is about two love affairs that were ended at the same time.

## THE CAMRY

There is an empty space in my garage
  that reminds me daily
  of the empty space in my life.
Her Toyota Camry filled that garage space.
But it was not just any Camry.
It was the metal and glass partner
  of a passionate love affair.
She had bought it some eight years ago,
  after exhaustive research and evaluations.
It was her first time buying her very own car,
  and she made it abundantly clear
  that she did not need my help.

Over the years,
  as she took care of her car,
  she did allow me to help
  with tire pressures and washer fluid,
  but nothing more.
She would handle the rest, and she did.
The car had more than its share
  of problems large and small,
  but they didn't seem to bother her.
The dealership knew of her great love,
  and treated her and the car with respect.
She always forgave the car
  and did not withhold her love,
  much the way she treated her children.

During better times we joked
   about who might win
   if it came down to the Camry or me.
I was certain I would prevail, but there were
   times
   when I honestly thought the vote
   might be close.

I sold the car last week,
   two years after her illness
   kept her from driving,
   and ten months after she died.
Why did I keep it so long?
Because it meant so much to her,
   and thus was important to me.
It reminded me of better times,
   when she had her Camry,
   and she had me,
   and life was good.

## Christmas without Her

I approached the Christmas season trying hard not to anticipate what might happen and how I might feel, but rather just letting myself experience this first Christmas without her with no expectations and no fears. The kids would be home and that guaranteed there would be some laughter in the house, even as we all missed Patty. I decided to put up the artificial tree, put the candle lights in the outside windows, and arrange all of the other decorations we had previously used throughout the house, including the kids' stockings by the fireplace. It cheered me up and was a welcome change from the previous year when the laughter and the decorations were missing.

Christmas time passed easily for us with much less sorrow than I might have expected. Of course it helped that the previously mentioned Mike and Jane adopted my family into theirs for a memorable Christmas day that helped us feel connected.

New Years Eve, however, was another story. With the kids gone back to their Chicago lives, I went to some good friends' home, along with couples I knew well and some that I didn't. It turned out to not be a good fit for me. The others' long established familiarity with each other led to merriment that I just could not handle at this point in my life. I explained my situation to the hosts and left long before midnight. The tears started before I got out of their driveway and lasted all of the way home. Again, the unpredictability of the grieving process had jumped up. But I was not afraid of it. I understood it, and I took care of myself the only

179

way I could. I sent an apology the next day, telling them how much I appreciated their thoughtfulness to include me. It wasn't really needed. They understood.

New Years Day brought yet another twist. I was invited to the home of some long time friends, along with the oft mentioned Mike and Jane. I felt so at home there in a small group, with quiet conversation, a great meal, and a Michigan Rose Bowl victory. It was just what I needed.

The Christmas season turned out to be yet another new adventure on the healing road. And simple events moved me to write.

## AVE MARIA

I played my Christmas music today.
It is a tape I made years ago
  of all my favorite hymns;
  old time classics like
  "O Holy Night,"
  "Away In A Manger"
  and "O Come All Ye Faithful."
But my favorite is first on the tape,
  and it is played the most.
The title is simply "Ave Maria"
  and it is the most beautiful work
  that I have ever heard
Isaac Stern plays it quite simply,
  coaxing violin strains that are so pure
  my heart soars with each phrase,
  until I can feel His presence
  with His mother
  in my little space on earth.
I don't know why this music affects me so.
I could not even tell you
  which composer's version I am
  listening to.
But it makes no difference.
My heart doesn't care.


I feel obligated to point out
  that I have no extreme devotion to Mary.

My connection has always been with her Son.
So this music's effect on me is a mystery,
    not so easily defined, but so very real.
Why it grips me so is not really important.
The only thing that matters is the effect.
And when I hear the violin sing "Ave Maria"
    I am transported briefly to a better place.
My everyday world stops for a time,
    while my mind works its special magic.
The music expands to fill my consciousness
    with purity,
    with hope,
    and with love.
That is the power of music.
That is the gift
    of the One
    whose birthday we celebrate.

## CHRISTMAS CARDS

The cards stream in daily now
    as Christmas draws near.
Since I am alone I am more eager
    for any mail to keep me company.
Christmas cards are special.
They tell me that good people care,
    that they are remembering me.
But sometimes the card troubles me.
Sometimes the message is too cheerful
    for this place where I find myself today.
They write on the colorful card,
    "We wish you the joy of the season," or
    "Wishing you a very merry Christmas," or
    "Best wishes for a wonderful Christmas
    and a happy New Year."
These people knew my Patty.
Do they want to chase my pain away
    with their happy words?
Do they think that real happiness is possible
    this first Christmas since she's gone?
Don't they know that each day I struggle
    just to keep my balance,
    and that this first Christmas alone,
    after thirty five together,
    is the worst time of all?
I want to scream at them,
    "Don't tell me to be joyous.

Tell me instead
>   how much you loved my Patty and
>   miss her,
>   how you understand my pain,
>   how you will pray for me,
>   and wish me His comfort."
There are knowing souls who do this.
Some have grieved also at Christmas,
>   others are just very wise.
But I should not be upset
>   at those who don't know what I need.
The important thing is that they care,
>   and that they want me to be what I was
>   before she went away.
In the past I wanted the same for those like me,
>   and didn't want to face their grief.
That was before I learned that pain and loss
>   must be openly shared by those
>   who love.

## THE PLAQUE

*Chicago Hope* was a favorite show of ours.
We liked the very human stories and people.
Now that she's gone I watch it alone.
It helps me feel connected to her, and to life.
Tonight the show wasn't really about doctors,
          or nurses, or even medicine.
It was simply about fathers and sons,
          and the love born of blood
          that can sometimes go bad.
As I watched the story unfold
          thoughts of parenting filled my head.
I too have a son, along with two daughters.
They are adults now, and quite simply,
          the greatest joys of my life.
On a Christmas day a few years ago
          they gave me a beautiful plaque,
          inscribed with words from their hearts
          that made me so very proud.
Their words said, "You have shown us
          a sincere and loving way to live,
          and therefore to this world
          we have much more to give."
Could there be a better tribute?
Am I a lucky father?
The fathers on TV were not so fortunate.
Their sons were separated from them,
          with little chance of reconciliation.

185

Those fathers had no plaques on their walls.
I cried for them and for their sons.
Their pain was so real and,
     since she's gone,
     I know well the pain of separation.
But my tears were a little different.
For mixed in with the sad ones
     were  tears of joy,
     because I have a beautiful plaque
     hanging proudly on my wall
     that says I did my fathering well,
     and that I am dearly loved.
It is quite simply
     the finest Christmas present
     that I have ever received.

## THE CHRISTMAS PRESENT

It was her last Christmas present,
    and she never loved one more.
When her life was nearing its end,
    even as others were rejoicing
    with the glitter and merriment
    of another holiday season,
    she devised a plan
    to make the most
    of her last Christmas.
She would have special friends in
    for a farewell visit.
But there was a big problem.
She had no proper bed jacket.
And while the disease could sap her strength
    and damage her spirit,
    her pride was untouched.
She must look her best for her visitors.
So Santa Claus and his helper Laura
    were dispatched to the shopping war zone.
They returned with a jacket
    of pink, white lace and the softness
    of angels' wings.
When the friends came
    they all had to know of her special present,
    admire the beauty, and feel the softness.
Men and women alike all had to participate
    as her eyes lit up and her smile widened
    with the small portion of joy left to her

She loved her bed jacket
and I think it must have reminded her
of the good things she had known.

When our loved one leaves us
and the heavy sorrow descends,
the future is at best uncertain,
and at worst dark and lonely.
So we look to find a small bit of light
to help us find our way.
During this first Christmas without her,
I will look at her bed jacket.
I will eye the pink and lace,
feel the unearthly softness,
and I will remember.
And she will be there.

## Thanks, Especially for the Light

I had always been a believer in giving thanks to the Almighty. And since I had received so much during my lifetime, the thanking became a daily ritual. Could I still do this, in the midst of my grieving over the greatest loss of my life? The answer, as it had been all during her ordeal, was a resounding yes.

With the beginning of 1998 came the usual dark period for Michigan. And for the first time that I could remember it seemed to really bother me. Previously only Patty was affected. She was well aware of seasonal affective disorder even before scientists determined it was real and gave it a name. When she was well she would rush around the house in the morning, opening blind and turning or lights. I, on the other hand, had no such mood problems with the dark periods and would often be reading the paper and having breakfast in semi-darkness when she arrived to admit the light and question whether I was part mushroom. That changed however when she died Now I was the one so aware of the darkness, so affected in my mood. I rushed around as soon as I got up to let in the light. And of course, on a particularly bright day after a string of gloomy days, I wrote.

## THANKS

Each night, before I go to sleep,
    I get down on my knees
    and give thanks to my God
    for all of the blessings I have been given.
I have been performing this ritual
    since I was a very small child.
Sometimes, when I am playing tennis,
    the game that is my great passion,
    I will, after a particularly great shot,
    pick out a white cloud,
    or, if indoors,
    one of the bright lights,
    and will pray a silent thank you
    for the gifts of health and opportunity.
It is not so easy to do
    when the shots are not there for me,
    but I still try to remember the thanks.
When my Patty was ill,
    I gave thanks for what we had been given,
    before I asked for courage, strength
    and acceptance
    for her and for me.
Why do I do it?
Probably part faith,
    part duty,
    and part habit.
I do know that it has worked quite well for me.

I am certainly beholden
    to this higher Eternal Power
    that I believe in, without fully
    understanding.
And I do recognize
    how richly I have been blessed.
So I will continue to offer my thanks,
    on my knees and on the court,
    because He has given me so much,
    and I also have a big match this Saturday.

## LIGHT

I feel so much better today,
        and there is no good reason for it.
She is still gone.
I am still alone.
My future is no more clear.
But the sun is shining,
        and that is the difference.
The whole world looks better to me.
My step is livelier.
I hear a song in my mind.
I am able to smile.
It is as if my God decided
        that I had been too gray,
        my spirit too closely matching
        the leaden skies
        and the damp chill of the air
        that had penetrated my core,
        where the coldness of loss
        already resided.
This all knowing God
        spoke directly to my soul,
        reminding me through His light
        that there was still joy
        in the kingdom,
        if I would only search it out.
The sun would be my sign,
        the rest would be up to me.

When she was with me
> the dark days of winter
> did not affect me as much.

I guess I had enough light
> in my life
> to combat dreary days.

Now I need to work harder
> to fight the darkness,
> to remember the light,
> to find the joy.

And the sunshine reminds me
> that I have assistance from
> the very creator of light,
> Who is the Light.

**God's Place Called Heaven, Ours Called Earth, and More**

In early February I traveled to California to visit with long time friends in San Pedro and San Diego. There was much to see and do, and the caring that I felt from my hosts was indeed welcome. I didn't expect to write on the trip but that strange mental sidekick of mine put ideas into my head that needed to find expression. Once again the healing process was at work, this time producing ideas somewhat separate from the grieving, but also connected by spirituality, love of the land, light, and uncertainty.

## HEAVEN

I don't really like to travel.
I tend to get nervous.
I'm much more comfortable at home,
    surrounded by the familiar.
But on those occasions when I fly,
    things change in a hurry.
When the plane breaks through the clouds
    and the total blue of the sky
    covers the puffy white below,
    I feel closer to God
    and his promised land.
It is childish for sure.
God and heaven aren't "up."
But in that moment I don't care.
The glory of our existence
    is that we can take our mind
    on journeys of our own choosing.
No extra charge.
No waiting.
No crowds.
And if I want to dream without sleeping,
    why not?
And if I want to look 'up' to find Patty
    enjoying the first year of her spirit life,
    why not?
Some advertisers would have us believe

that "Image is everything."
But their image has a price tag.
Mine is free,
    with as many replays as I want.
So I'll continue to dream
    in my window seat,
    as I hurtle across the country.
And if another passenger wonders
    about my knowing smile
    that has appeared suddenly
    I won't care.
I know where I am.
I know where she is.
And I still like to think it's "up."

## THE LAND

From 30,000 feet I see the canyons
    and the mighty Colorado river.
The shadow of the plane
    crosses lands unspoiled
    since creation.
Colors fill my being,
    the deep blue of the water,
    the multi-hued grays and browns
    of the land.
The plane is strangely quiet,
    with only a low hum audible.
But I hear something else,
    and it reverberates in my head.
I hear the land,
    and it is speaking directly to me
    in strident tones.
It is warning me away.
"Do not spy on me from above," it shouts.
"Do not mark my hills
    and the path of the great water
    from your place in the sky.
You cannot find my being there.
You must paddle my rivers,
    with their unspoiled banks
    and clear water.
You must walk the land
    and feel the pulse of its life,

        still yourself and listen
        to the sounds of my creatures,
        lie down under the stars
        and witness magnificence.
I am here for you.
I want to hold you close to me,
        feel your heartbeat against mine,
        know that you love me
        and will care for me,
        always."

## PLEASE TALK TO ME

She sits in the corner booth, alone.
I can't help but notice her
    as I work through my breakfast
    and the morning newspaper.
Since I too am alone
    on vacation in a new city,
    I am more alert to her,
    and I have the time
    to observe and listen.
Since Patty's death left me alone,
    I seem to be more aware of others
    alone without partners.
She appears to be in her seventies,
    hastily dressed with little makeup.
I would guess she lives alone,
    and does not need to please another.
She is obviously a regular here,
    unhappy that her "regular girl"
    is not working today.
She is fussy about her order,
    wanting everything just so,
    as older folks often do.
But there is much more going on.
She summons her server too often,
    and holds her in conversation
    much too long.

The server is patient with her,
    learning more than she needs to know.
I hear only bits and pieces,
    about sons who live far away,
    about the weather,
    about her regular server.
There seems to be some desperation
    in her pointless rambling.
I marvel at the patience of the server,
    who gives the lady her attention
    in the midst of her busiest time.
I decide that the lady is very lonely,
    a harmless judgement
    with a troubling afterthought.
I hope that I will never have to be
    the lonely person
    in the corner booth.

## LIGHT REVISITED

It was totally unexpected;
    rainstorms, overcast skies,
    and general gloom.
I certainly wasn't on vacation
    in southern California
    to experience the same dreadfulness
    that I had left in Michigan.
The first part of my vacation,
    visits with long time friends,
    was wonderful.
I felt so comfortable with them.
It reminded me of the good
    that was still present in my life,
    even though she was gone.
The rain was external,
    it did not reach my spirit,
    it did not interfere
    with the bonding.
But now I was on my own
    for five days
    in a San Diego
    that was reeling
    from the constant pounding
    of mother nature gone berserk.
After one day alone,
    I thought very seriously
    of heading for home

and the comfort of the known.
But then a magical thing happened,
just as it had a month before.
The sun appeared,
chasing away the gloom,
opening up a beautiful city
with so many delights.
I decided I would stay
for one more day,
then another,
and another.
God had found me again
and showed me His light,
told me He loved me,
just in case I had forgotten.

## An Anniversary Approaches

As I approached the anniversary of Patty's death I realized that there had been a barely noticed but nonetheless significant change in my grieving. I had moved to a different place, where my emotions were a little deeper under the surface. I was singing along with the radio tunes again, and actually thought about the dreaded "dating," seriously considering whether I wanted another relationship. I still had sad moments but it was different now. I wasn't devastated. The tears did not come as often and, when they did, they were much less traumatic. I did not know if this was some sort of temporary reprieve before another onslaught. After all, there are no rules for grieving, no "one size fits all." But nonetheless, the change was welcome and I determined that, like the entire previous year, I would let this stage unfold in its own way. In this respect I was continuing to follow the path which I had illuminated for myself some six months earlier when I wrote "Grieving."

## GRIEVING

It is as individual as a fingerprint,
    as unpredictable as a summer storm,
    as rocky as a roller coaster,
    and as pervasive as fine dust
    covering every inch of us.
It is called grief.

When our loved one dies,
    grief is born in us,
    confusing our mind,
    weakening our body,
    assaulting our senses,
    and wounding our spirit.
It will be our constant companion
    for a time not known.
We must welcome it,
    endure it,
    understand its importance,
    share it with those who love us,
    and learn from it.

From grieving we can learn
    that we are strong,
    that people are good
    and they want to help,
    that time is our ally,
    and that our life

will one day return to us,
offering the joy
that now eludes us,
and a heightened awareness
of its ultimate mystery.
But mostly we will learn
that the depth of our grief
is merely a reflection
of our God given humanity
and its awesome capacity
for love.

## Can You Believe It's Been a Year

Cathy and Laura came home to spend a few days with me leading up to February 18th, the first anniversary of Patty's death. I had told them that they didn't have to do it for me. But they said that they wanted to come. Doug was comfortable staying in Chicago.

The morning of the 18th was cold and rainy, exactly like the day a year ago when we said goodby to Patty in a church and then at the cemetery. Now the three of us returned to the cemetery, not knowing exactly what we would do or say. The rain had stopped by the time we stood at the grave site in the Good Shepherd Garden. It was still cold and the soggy ground was quickly making our feet wet. I wiped a few pieces of grass from the bronze that had been mostly cleaned by the rain. Not much was said as we stood there, each of us remembering her in our own way. I did comment on how much I liked that particular spot amidst the beautiful trees and the girls agreed. Soon it was time for them to head back to Chicago. As Cathy started for the car Laura lingered a bit. I asked her, "Are you OK?" She said, "Yes, I'm OK. How about you?" I replied, "I'm fine." So with that simple affirmation, we walked to the car and into year two.

That night, with the girls safely back in Chicago, I sat down to write a final poem to finish one year of grieving. But the words didn't come. The day had not been as emotional as I had expected. There had been no tears, and none of the ultra sharp memories that had been so much a part of the last year. Like most of my grieving time, the day took its own form and I lived it how

I felt it. I wondered why I did not feel more sadness on this anniversary day. But I knew that there was no answer for that question. I did know, however, that I had just completed the strangest year of my life; a year with more sadness, more soul searching, more love and more enlightenment than I could possibly have imagined.

## Year Two Begins and I Find More Hope

When I awoke on February 19th to begin a second year without her I was still a little puzzled about my reaction, or lack of it, at the cemetery. But by this time I had pretty much learned that the only predictable thing about grieving was the unpredictability. There was, however, no doubt that the world was looking much brighter to me.

During the next two months I had a burst of writing energy. And the words I wrote once again showed me how much I was healing. The poems mostly covered good memories and fond recollections, with some smiling accompanying the writing. I was getting a bit more excited about my life ahead.

One of the "good memory" poems was written as I thought about my older sister Rosemary, who died in 1996 after battling cancer for many years with amazing courage, grace, optimism and humor. When her birthday approached in March I wrote to celebrate her life, remembering what made her special and imagining what she might say to her family. I wrote it for the seven who called her mom and the many who called her grandma.

It was during this time period that I also stepped up my hospice volunteer activity, adding work with the bereavement support group. Once again I felt the workings of the divine plan that seems to crop up so often in these pages. Giving my time to help others who were grieving was paying huge dividends to me. I felt there was more purpose to my life and that I was contributing in an important way. I also discovered that helping them seemed to lift my own spirits, a marvelous byproduct of the sharing.

Of course, the general good cheer and optimism could always be interrupted by some sadness as the last offering will show. But again, these events were now far more isolated and of very brief duration.

## HER VOICE

I played a tape cassette
    the other day.
It was from 1991,
    during better times
    before the spread of the cancer
    that finally consumed her.
It was a session she had
    with a psychic,
    the kind of experience
    that she believed in
    as she searched
    for her rightful place
    in a complicated world.
The details are not important.
But the part where she laughed
    in a moment of pure joy
    is unforgettable.
This time I laughed with her
    in the privacy of my car.
For just a moment
    I too felt the joy,
    as I could almost feel her presence.

It was shortly after she died
    that I first found the tape.
On that occasion
    I only listened a moment

and didn't even get to the place
  with the wonderful laugh.
I was already crying
    and had to turn it off.
It just hurt too much.
But now it is different.
Time has once again
      worked its unique magic
      and softened me some,
      so that the sound of her voice
      can ease into my being
      and quietly awaken
      some of the good memories.
I am still wounded.
      but I am healing.

## CEMETERY REVISITED

I drive past the cemetery again,
    glancing at her spot
    among the familiar trees
    in the Good Shepherd Garden.
I say "Hi sweetie,"
    as I remember doing
    almost a year ago
    for the very first time,
    when I felt so much pain
    that the tears erupted.
This time it is different.
This time I actually smile.
I'm not really sure why.
Maybe it's because
    I actually feel some joy
    at knowing for sure
    that she is Home forever.
Maybe this thought
    is now enough to temper
    the ache of my emptiness.
Maybe it is just time
    working its peculiar magic
    and giving me a chance
    to cherish her memory,
    as I reach for the future.
It makes no difference
    why it is changed now.

It is only important
    that I can smile now,
    even as I miss her
    so terribly much.
    knowing that she
    is safe with Him,
    and that I am healing.

## LOVE STORY

I watched a TV movie today,
   to pass the time
   that I now have in abundance.
It was a simple story
   about real people,
   and how they handled love.
There was hopeful love,
   scared love,
   unsure love,
   distant love,
   and finally,
   the truest love.
Love stories
   have always reached me,
   but never more than now,
   when mine has been interrupted.
While she was with me,
   I thought I knew about love.
But I had so much to learn.
Grieving can be a great teacher,
   if you let the pain and the joy
   of the time together
   blend in the wonder of memories.
After a while
   the pain starts to ease
   and the good starts to grow,
   and with it the thought
   that it could happen again.

It doesn't have to of course.
Once may be enough,
    and there is no need to settle
    for anything less than real.
Just the barest idea
    that it could happen again
    is enough for now.
And isn't that the magic
    of a love story,
    found in an obscure movie,
    about real people
    just like me.

## THE MASTERS

I think that for a golfer
    it is quite simply
    the prettiest place on earth.
It is Augusta National,
    home of the Masters,
    where spring is welcomed
    with azalea, magnolia,
    and a carpet of unparalleled green,
    so perfect that footsteps
    seem an intrusion
    on God's private landscape.
Patty and I were lucky enough
    to visit some years ago,
    before the bad times came.
I do have a picture of her
    that I look at now and then
    when I feel the need
    for a good memory.
She is properly dressed
    for the sacred shrine of golf,
    resplendent in the bold colors
    and jaunty visor
    that were her trademark,
    and spoke loudly of who she was.
The spot chosen for the picture
    is absolutely magnificent,
    but forbidden to spectators,

a place where worshipers
    simply must not intrude.
I remember telling her
        that she could end up
        in an Augusta jail
        for such a serious crime.
And sure enough,
        out of nowhere came a guard
        to hasten us away.
We laughed about it then
It was so like her
        to challenge a rule
        that cried out for exception.
I smile just thinking about it.
I love that picture.

## THEATRE OF LIFE

I went to the theatre today,
    for the first time
    since she died.
It was *Chorus Line*,
    one of my favorites,
    and one of her favorites.
I remember long ago,
    standing in a huge line
    to get our tickets,
    feeling the excitement
    weeks before the show.
Theatre was one of those areas
    where we were "together"
    in our love.
A night at the theatre,
    with the attendant fancy dinner,
    was so very special.
We saw all of the top shows,
    and had dinner in the best places,
    thanks to an expense account.
That was part of the magic,
    when we didn't have much money.
Now I can afford theatre.
It's only one ticket,
    and the fancy dinners
    were really for her.
But I hadn't gone since she got sick,
    because I thought it strictly a
    doubles event,

until I read the morning paper
and chanced upon an article
about the university theatre group
and the last day of the Chorus Line run.
So I decided to go, telling myself
    that I was healing and that I could do it.
It felt strange in the theatre,
    listening to the buzz of voices,
    mostly couples,
    waiting for the curtain.
I felt awkward being alone.
Someone important was missing.
But that feeling ended
    when the darkness enfolded us
    and the stage came alive with dancing
The show captured me
    as I hoped it would.
I was suddenly involved
    with a group of dancers
    trying to live their dreams,
    fighting the long odds
    to dance in a chorus line.
My own life was put aside
    in the theatre of my mind,
    but only for two hours until the finale.
Then the eight dancers selected
    were resting in their happiness,
    discussing their choice
    of such a difficult life,
    with heartbreak always

just a "Sorry, we can't use you,"
or, "Bad news, the show is folding" away.
They then sang "What I Did for Love."
Suddenly I was with them,
thinking their thoughts
about the roadblocks life presents
to following a dream,
and how they did it purely for love.
I too was in the theatre for a long time,
because I loved it, and because
I loved her.
It was the theatre of life and marriage.
I was part of an ensemble
that had a thirty four year run,
playing in two states,
from a tiny second story walk-up,
to a large, beautiful colonial,
realistic in every sense.
Our story line changed over the years,
as the script was revised
to include new talent.
The newcomers stayed for much of the run,
but then left for their own "Broadway."
Our play was very successful,
ignored for public awards
but an artistic success.
Then came the dreaded news.
The show must close.
The female lead had left
for a much better part
in a far more beautiful theatre.

## ACADEMY AWARDS

I watched the *Academy Awards* tonight.
As usual the show was exciting,
    and ran far too long.
This was the first year
    that I can remember watching alone.
Patty and I were movie fans.
It was one of those areas,
    like raising our children,
    where we were in beautiful sync.
When we went to the movies
    and got settled in the comfy darkness,
    we left the world outside
    for a couple of hours.
We would both be caught up
    in others' lives, loves,
    joys, and heartbreaks.
We would always hold hands
    for part of the time,
    reinforcing our closeness
    and shared enjoyment.
The love of the movies
    naturally led to a love
    of the annual awards show.
Last year was actually
    my first *Academy Awards* without her.
I don't even know if I watched.
It was so close to her passing

from the theatre of life
that the days were mostly a blur.
So I'll count this year as number one
and present the first ever Oscar
to Patty Gries,
in the brand new category,
Best Actual Life Performance
by a Female Lead
in an Original Production
Based on a True Story
of a Life Well Lived.
"Congratulations, Patty,
and if you wouldn't mind,
we're running a little late here,
so please just share your acceptance
with the other stars in eternity."

## MY TEACHER

She taught me much about our life,
    this wife I held so dear.
There wasn't much she didn't know,
    and nothing she did fear.

While I might often hesitate
    when trying something new,
    she'd forge ahead with not a thought
    that it could go askew.

She knew the names of flowers and plants,
    and what things helped them grow.
She must have spent one life a plant,
    for all that she did know.

She knew her colors and how they worked,
    with subtle shade and hue,
    while I knew black, white, brown and
    green,
    and of course red, white and blue.

She didn't let our chosen Church
    dictate how she must find
    the righteous way to life with God,
    for didn't SHE form her mind?

And what of women and their rights
to share in equal measure.
There was so much I needed to know,
it gave her so much pleasure.

Her lessons covered kitchen skills,
and laundry where I was less sure.
In fact the laundry skills she taught
might be my greatest treasure.

My mind saw just one way to fold,
deviation was for the birds.
You folded in half and half again,
but her wisdom taught me "thirds."

## FROM ROSEMARY WITH LOVE

It will be my birthday soon.
If I were still with you
    we would be celebrating it
    as number sixty seven.
But in the place where I am
    years do not matter,
    for all of time is mightily blessed.
If I could visit with you again
    on my special day,
I would ask you to do these things
    in memory of me.

Let your love shine brightly,
    for it is a miraculous gift
    that is only increased with use
    by the Source of all love.
It is in the loving
    and the sharing of ourselves
    that we become one with Him.

Laugh often and heartily,
    for it is indeed a balm
    that awakens the senses,
    soothes the spirit,
    lightens the load,
    and spreads joy
    throughout the kingdom.

And if the laugh is on you,
    enjoy it just as much,
    for we are all funny creatures.


Work hard and for the right reasons.
There is nothing more noble
    than an honest effort
    that provides a fair return
    and promotes the common good.
Try to find a life's work
    that you truly enjoy,
    for you will be spending
    much of your life at it.


Cry when you need to,
    when the sadness of life
    finds and fills your heart.
The tears are cleansing
    and soothing.
With our tears
    we join and support
    those who suffer
    in our common brotherhood.


Give generously of yourselves
    with your money and your time,
    for there will always be those
    who need a helping hand
    or a listening ear,
    or just a smile and a hug.

And lastly, pray.
Pray often and deeply,
    for that is how your God
    wishes to talk to you
    and listen to you.
He will show you the way
    and He will answer your prayer,
    but not always in the way
    that you might expect.
Sometimes you will not understand
    how your prayer is answered
    because you do not yet know,
    as I do now,
    how the power of God
    works wondrously on earth.

This is what I ask of you,
    the ones I love,
    as I celebrate my special day
    in this most special of places.

CREAM OF WHEAT

Is it possible to write a poem
      about a bowl of Cream of Wheat?
It is if you made it today
      for only yourself,
      and it made you cry.

Cream of Wheat
      was all that she could eat
      for the last part of her life.
First with apple juice,
      a slice of white toast
      buttered hot
      with Spoon Fruit jam,
      delivered on a tray
      to her dying place.
Later the toast disappeared,
      as her throat hurt.
Then the juice tasted bad.
Finally, the portions
      of the Cream of Wheat
      were reduced,
      as appetite waned,
      and the act of eating
      became far too difficult.
Then the eating stopped.

As I ate my Cream of Wheat,
      alone in the big house,

I wished for more days
> when I could make it for her.
There are things I wanted to tell her
>> while she ate,
>> and I read something funny
>> that might have coaxed a tiny smile.
But those days are over,
>> except for the memories
>> and I'm doing better every day.
I just don't think
>> that I'll make
>> Cream of Wheat again,
>> at least for awhile

## I've Run Out of Poems but Not Words

At this point, fourteen months after she died, I believe that I am well along the healing path with the worst behind me. So I will interrupt my poem writing and conclude, but not without offering some last thoughts. I would be remiss if I didn't include a brief section summarizing some things that I discovered through this very painful process. They are covered in no particular order for I believe them all to be important. Although they are particular to my experience, I believe they are universal in application and hope that some of them might be helpful.

Self Forgiveness — It is a truism that if we don't love ourselves we cannot love others. And a large part of love is forgiveness, for we are all so very human and imperfect. The strain of serious illness can produce unique conflict and disagreements that we might not be prepared for. So it is important that we learn to say, "I'm sorry," to any that we might have hurt. And then we must forgive ourselves and move on. This will also be important during grieving when at times we might be troubled, wondering if we did enough, and can no longer say, "I'm sorry." The answer, hopefully, is that we did the best that we could with who we were at that time and what we were facing, and never stopped trying to do better.

Assistance — There is help available for those with end of life and grief issues. For us it was hospice who provided such compassionate care for the last months of Patty's life. I cannot say enough about the medical, emotional, and spiritual support we received, support that continued after she died. I will say it once more, in case there is any question about how I feel—HOSPICE! And now I'll mention two publications that occupy a prominent place on my kitchen table. The first is *Daily Word*, a publication of the Unity School of Christianity in Unity Village, MO. (1-800-669-0282). They provide a monthly pamphlet with concise daily readings of the most positive nature. Their message encompasses the universal brotherhood of man in harmony with the love of God and His wondrous plan for each of us. For me it has proven to be a major blessing. Another publication, which I heartily recommend for the grieving, is the book *Healing After Loss* by Martha Whitmore Hickman. (Avon Books, 1-800-238-0658). This book also provides short daily readings that put the grieving process in wonderful perspective. Many of the readings were a total revelation to me, explaining why I was so troubled at times, sharing others feelings so similar to mine, and offering always the promise of healing. There are words of consolation and hope from the famous and the ordinary, along with a beautiful collection of ideas on coping.

The Goodness of Man and Woman — My experience with caregiving and grieving has produced so much of the good in people that at times I have been overwhelmed. It has led to many of the writings in this book. And it has also directed me to what I believe to be a universal truth—love is everywhere if we only let it into our lives and try to be more open in sharing. In these pages you have met courageous people who fight the ravages of disease with grace and dignity, and caring people who know how to listen and how to love. Their example challenges and inspires me.

<u>Don't Forget To Write</u> — Here I am, nearing the end, and I nearly forgot one of the most important ingredients to managing caregiving and grief—personal writing. Again, this is not an original idea. Learned people have been recommending journal writing for a long time as a way to get in touch with the feelings that drive us. To me it makes no difference what form the writing takes. I chose poems because it allowed me to focus on a particular idea or event while it was very fresh. The important thing is that the writing reflect the feelings. Why the process works is a bit of a mystery to me. But I have learned that recording my feelings does in fact bring a certain clarity to them that does not come just from thinking. Perhaps the extra thought needed to put words to the ideas somehow forces us to dig a little deeper. For me, that digging often allowed me to learn much about myself that might have stayed hidden. If I was to do the best possible job of taking care of Patty, and later myself, I needed to know who I was dealing with. The writing told me.

<u>It's the Journey that Counts</u> — If there is one idea that has been totally reinforced in my mind during the difficult years of caregiving and grieving it is the concept of life as a journey. Yes, I believe there is a goal, and it is everlasting and wondrous. But getting there can involve as many paths as there are people, and a time frame equally personal. For Patty the journey was a little less than fifty six years, almost two thirds of which I shared. Her journey was uniquely hers, filled with wondrous achievement. The last four years of that journey offered the opportunity for the expression of every possible human emotion, as an entire lifetime was remembered in the face of  much suffering. Never has it been

more clear to me how much value is found in each person's journey, and how important we are to each other as we travel our individual paths to the place of togetherness. I wish that I had been more "aware" before I began sharing Patty's ordeal. It would have helped if I had had more understanding of the things that were happening to her and to me. But my journey needed to take a particular turn for me to learn what I needed to know. I'm not sure what it was that put a pencil in my hand just at the right time. But I do know that from the experiencing came the writing, from the writing came the learning, and from the learning came the sharing.

In reviewing the material for this book I came across a letter I wrote to my kids in 1992, more than a year before our journey would take such a remarkable turn. I think that I was already being given some help from above by the witnessing of a baby's short but meaningful life. It is almost as if I was getting a personal message that would help me in the upcoming struggle. I share it in the hope that others may look for the value in each and every journey.

Dear Cathy, Doug and Laura
March 12, 1992

I went to Julie McGlynn's baby's funeral today and the experience was so worthwhile that I decided I had to write this note and tell you about it. In case you don't know the details, the baby was born seven months ago with heart problems that were very serious and would necessitate a series of operations. The first open heart surgery last week was thought to be successful but there were complications and, a few days later, the baby died.

I thought the funeral experience would be extremely sad and a real downer. Much to my surprise I found the service to be very much uplifting, with an emphasis on the value every life brings to us and the reward when God calls our name. To see the many relatives and friends gathered to offer support, and to share the Eucharist with them, was truly inspiring. Father Tocco's homily was comforting in focusing on life as a journey whose length is unpredictable, but whose destination is everlasting peace and joy with our Creator.

So it is not with a heavy heart that I send this message. Yes, I'm sad at the baby's death and I sympathize with the parents' and relatives' grief. But I am also renewed in my faith that there is purpose to our time on earth, no matter how long that is. Many lives were affected by this baby who only had seven months. Whether seven months, or eighty seven years like grandma, it is an important journey to be lived to the fullest possible and then to result in the everlasting reward.

Well, I didn't mean to be so preachy, but I did want to communicate my thoughts to you. Each of you is on a journey to your Creator. If you look at life in those terms it might help during the tough times. And, as I'm sure you know, tough times are definitely a part of the journey for all of us.

My thoughts and prayers are always with you on your journey.

Love,
Dad

## I'm Done and Wondering Why I Did This

Well, that's it. This is the last section. It is time to conclude and move on. I'm glad I wrote when I did about what happened to us. It was necessary for me to sort everything out in order to better handle it. But even as I finish and try to find out if the book has any merit, I wonder why I did it. It was not for money. I decided before I began putting it together that I would not profit even a penny from it. It is just not that kind of book. Why would I share so much of myself when, for most of my life, I have been unsure enough to keep my life mostly private? And do I really think anyone cares about the personal trials of one person out of legions who have followed a similar path? Again, I don't know for sure. But there are some important things that I learned these past years. And one of the most important is the responsibility I feel to share myself and my experience with others. I learned that all of us are much more alike than we are different, especially in seeking the love that governs everything. I learned from the responses of others who have sampled my poems that my thoughts, which always seemed so unique to me, and sometimes a little strange, are shared by countless others. I learned that if you allow others into your life when the going gets tough you will more often than not be overwhelmed with their caring. But I think the largest lesson for me, who for many reasons has led a life with much uncertainty, and even fear, is simply that I do not have to fear whatever this life has in store for me. In five very difficult years I learned that I could survive the greatest trial and the greatest loss of my life with help from above and below. And not only could I survive—I could even grow as a person and become stronger, more aware of life's mystery and purpose, and more thankful for the God given opportunity to be alive. It is a lesson painfully learned and hopefully shared.

# Epilogue

There is one more poem, written long after the book material was selected, that continues the story of my personal transformation.

## CHANGED FOREVER

I am changed forever.
I know it for sure now.
No more can I look at life
    without seeing deep inside it,
    without experiencing so much
    in the simple nature of it.
Her suffering and death
    opened up my being
    so that the sights and sounds
    of my everyday life
    sometimes seem enlarged tenfold.
The emotional content
    grips the very fabric of my life,
    awakening me to its majesty
    and ultimate mystery.
I cannot turn my back or this.
I know there is purpose to it,
    though my path is not always clear.
I have been given more years
    to remember her,
    and to honor that memory.
There are many who need me,
    in ways that I may not even know.
But I do know that I can help.
And I simply can't say no.